TUNING THE MUSICIAN'S HEART

VOL.2, JULY-DECEMBER

Garen L. Wolf I

Chairman Emeritus, Division of Music,
God's Bible School and College,
Cincinnati, Ohio

Author of
Music of the Bible in Christian Perspective
Church Music Matters
Music Philosophy in Christian Perspective

SCHMUL PUBLISHING COMPANY
NICHOLASVILLE, KENTUCKY

Published by Schmul Publishing Co.
PO Box 776
Nicholasville, KY 40340
USA

ISBN 10: 0-88019-636-X
ISBN 13: 978-0-88019-636-9

Visit us on the Internet at www.wesleyanbooks.com, or
order direct from the publisher by calling 800-772-6657, or
by writing to the above address.

Contents

This book is
DEDICATED
to the memory of my mother

ANNA MAYME POTTER WOLF
1914-2009

My mother represented God to me from the time that I was a small child. She was also one of the greatest positive influences in my life as I was growing up. She not only talked about God to me often, but she also talked often to God about me. I am convinced that I am a Christian today because of God's wonderful grace and mercy and my mother's faithfulness at the place of prayer. It is with great joy and certainty that I assert that she fought a good fight, finished her course, kept the faith and is now enjoying the things that the Lord, the righteous judge, has prepared for her. It is my prayer that those who come behind me will find me as faithful as my godly mother was to me.

Acknowledgement

I want to thank Deanna Mander who was the content editor and also gave me enduring support and patience as I prepared this work.

Introduction

Why I Prepared This Devotional Collection

THERE ARE A NUMBER of excellent devotional works to be found online and in print today. So, I gave much thought to the development of this collection before I set out to prepare 365 devotionals specifically written for musicians. My goal was to capture many of my former devotional thoughts and to deal with current concerns of Christian musicians.

Serving Jesus Christ is not always "hippity hop over the top" but sometimes a titanic spiritual struggle. This collection includes joy, sadness, depression, misunderstanding, commitment and a host of my thoughts of praise to the wonderful God that I love and serve. As I set out to prepare this material, I purposed in my heart to deal with real problems and situations that Christian musicians encounter in the context of their musical ministry. Because these devotional thoughts many times include current philosophical concerns, the devotions are often of a philosophical nature.

It would have been much easier to prepare these devotionals as if musicians were always happy, successful and ministering in an atmosphere devoid of misunderstanding and pressure. However, this is seldom the case. So, in the midst of this conflict, they can struggle to have a good attitude, to show a right spirit and live a victorious, Christlike life.

As I worked on this devotional collection, I often thought of the words of the hymn *Our Great Savior*, "tempted, tried and sometimes failing, He, my strength, my victory wins." The topics mentioned above have been a reality in my spiritual journey, and during the times of doubt and failure, Christ has been my strong tower and source of victory. Also, I must confess that my spiritual "harp" is prone to getting out of tune and therefore, I need to tune it regularly. Over the years I have found that it doesn't make much sense for me to try to tune my "harp" until I have tuned my heart.

This collection of past and present devotional thoughts will possibly bring a smile, chuckle, and a tear to the many former choir and Symphonic Wind and String Ensemble members who remember me standing at the front of the "Big Bus" sharing many of these devotional thoughts as we traveled each morning to a new ministry opportunity. *Soli Deo Gloria!*

Why I Include Transliterations and Strong's Numbers

Many music directors and music educators have not had the opportunity to study Greek, Hebrew and biblical Aramaic while they were in an undergraduate or graduate music degree program in college. For this reason I do not write any of the Bible language words and/or definitions in Hebrew, Aramaic or Greek characters. There is a multitude of Bible study books that include the keyed numbers found in *Strong's Exhaustive Concordance*. Because I include Strong's keyed numbers, those who read my philosophical writings have an immediate connection to scholarly sources which are keyed to *Strong's Concordance* without the hassle of having to compare the characters of the Hebrew, Aramaic or Greek words that are found in the many Bible study works.

I often read books and periodical articles by authors who contend that a passage of Scripture has a certain meaning, but when I study it, I cannot substantiate that it has the meaning that an author purports. It would be a significant help if all authors would identify exactly which Hebrew, Aramaic, or Greek word is being referenced by using Strong's keyed numbers, and transliterate the words for the reader who is not able to read the original biblical languages.

All words found in any language have meaning based on how they are used in sentences. Words mean something, and the writers of Scripture, who were inspired to write sentences under the direct (plenary) inspiration of the Holy Spirit, wrote exactly what they meant to say. It does not make any sense to suppose that an inspired writer of Scripture would have used words that meant exactly what he did not intend to say. Misunderstandings of Scripture are most often the result of the reader not having a grasp of the original language, an understanding of the meaning of the words, or an understanding of how the inspired writers used these words in the context of writing Scripture.

When I commit my beliefs to pen and ink, it is possible that I spend more time with the English dictionary, Bible language dictionaries, and lexicons than I do writing. My writings are far from inspired, but that does not mean that I do not labor over each word, phrase and sentence. I would be greatly offended if my readers were to suppose that I had intended to write the opposite meaning of my words.

So, if a writer expects readers to trust his supposed meanings of the original Bible words in his writings, that author must treat the ancient inspired writings of the Old and New Testaments with much respect. Changing the Holy Writ to merely fit modern thinking is a very dangerous writing technique. As Revelation 22:18, 19 warns, "For I testify unto every man that heareth the words of the prophecy of this book, If any man shall add unto these things, God shall add unto him the plagues that are written in this book: And if any man shall take away from the words of the book of this prophecy, God shall take away his part out of the book of life, and out of the holy city, and from the things which are written in this book." Therefore, a writer has an obligation to the original meaning of the inspired words that were used in the Bible. When I am exposing and defining original passages of the Bible that are thousands of years old, I endeavor to always identify the original words, as well as give keyed numbers, so that the reader has help to do personal language studies to establish whether my interpretations are valid or not.

Although I have used Strong's keyed numbers and some of his definitions in the preparation of this book, I did not always use them in their entirety because they do not always take into consideration the context of a particular Scripture passage and other historical considerations that sometimes influence the meaning of words. For these reasons I have used the definitions found in various lexicons, dictionaries and other sources that have included language study.

Why I Use Lexical Forms of Words

As I mentioned earlier, many Church musicians and Christian music educators do not read Greek, Hebrew or Aramaic. For this reason I have chosen to include in my writings the lexical forms of the words (except in direct quotes of other authors) and their keyed numbers found in *Strong's Concordance*. A lexical form is an abstract unit representing a set of word forms differing only in inflection and not in core meaning. Bible lexicons provide definitions and meaning of Biblical words found in the original Greek, Hebrew, and Aramaic languages used in the Bible. Lexicons help those who do Bible word studies to understand the origins and root meaning of the ancient languages used in the Bible. Lexicons often give the context and cultural meaning intended by the authors of the Bible.

When a student who does not know how to read Greek, Hebrew, or Aramaic is reading an English translation of the Bible, the only way to find out what a particular word means in the original language is to look it up in a lexicon. Lexicons use what is called "lexical forms of words" which means that this language source deals with the vocabulary of a language rather than with grammatical and syntactical aspects. The grammatical and syntactical aspects are largely determined by context. Ultimately, words only have exact meaning in the context in which they are used. A lexicon or dictionary only gives the range of possible meanings.

About the Use of Scripture

There are over 600 references to music that are found in the Bible. These scriptures have made it possible for the serious music minister and music educator to have a great amount of guidance in the development of a music philosophy and praxis. However, it is a mistake to suppose that these aforementioned direct references to music and musicing are the only verses in the Bible that have meaning in the development of a Christocentric music philosophy or in a Christian musician's life.

Every Christian musician must remember that he or she is a Christian first and a musician second. For this reason it is necessary to include Bible verses that do not mention music and musicians but, because they are germane to living a Christian life, are essential when a Christian musician is developing his or her worldview.

Symbols and Abbreviations

AV — Authorized King James Version, the KJV.

ASV — American Standard Version.

Ibid. — The abbreviation for *ibidem*, which means "a further reference to a work which was just cited."

KJV — King James Version, the AV.

Kosmos — Words like this are transliterations of Hebrew, Aramaic, and Greek words used in the Bible. They are an attempt to spell out these words literally in English.

LORD — English translations of the Bible generally use this in place of the tetragrammaton (see below). It differentiates for the common use of "Lord" or "lord" in other contexts. For the sake of reverence of the Holy Name, I use it also in the text of this book.

NIV — New International Version.

NKJV — New King James Version.

NT — New Testament. This abbreviation does not refer to any version of the Bible.

OT — Old Testament. This abbreviation does not refer to any version of the Bible.

YHVH — (also *YHWH*) This tetragrammaton is of uncertain pronunciation since it was not pronounced by the ancient Jewish community for centuries because it was considered to be too sacred to be pronounced. Therefore, the vowel sounds are now uncertain. It was translated Jehovah by the King James scholars and as YHWH, YHVH, Yawveh, Yahweh or Yahovah by others.

Foreword

ALL MUSICIANS KNOW that tuning is a vital element of successful musicianship. This book admonishes Christian musicians to put as much care into tuning their heart to the voice of God, as the tuning of their instrument before performing.

This book is a collection of devotionals that my father has given over his many years of music ministry. As one of his students, my ears still ring with the devotional that began with, "I beseech you therefore, brethren, by the mercies of God, that you present your bodies a living sacrifice… which is your reasonable [or rational] service." In this book you will find that devotional along with other inspiring favorites such as, "In the year king Uzziah died," "Desert Pete" and "Spiritual Horticulture."

Whether you had an opportunity to study under him or not, this book offers encouragement and challenge to all Christian musicians. It is simply a musician sharing his heart and passion for music ministry. He speaks with the authority of someone who faithfully studies what the Bible says about being a Christian musician. His wisdom and stories beckon the musician to choose joy, gratitude and full surrender to Christ.

Let this devotional book challenge you to study what the Bible says about music and being a musician. As you read it, you will find that it is written from the author's heart, reminding us that God cares about music and God cares about the musician. The spirit of these devotionals reveal what has guided and spiritually sustained Garen Wolf through a lifetime of music ministry.

—DEANNA (WOLF) MANDER
Editor

JULY

July 1

I'm a Servant Who Has Been Forgiven

Ephesians 2:1-9 — "And you did he make alive, when ye were dead through your trespasses and sins, wherein ye once walked according to the course of this world... we also all once lived in the lusts of our flesh, doing the desires of the flesh and of the mind, and were by nature children of wrath, even as the rest:— but God, being rich in mercy, for his great love wherewith he loved us, even when we were dead through our trespasses, made us alive together with Christ... for by grace have ye been saved through faith; and that not of yourselves, it is the gift of God; not of works, that no man should glory." (ASV)

Verses one through nine explain to all Christian musicians who we *were* and who we now *are* through God's love and grace. We were dead and are now alive because Christ has forgiven us from our trespasses and sins. This has become a reality in our lives because Christ has saved us by His grace. The phrase "the course (*aion* 165) of this world (*kosmos* 2889)" used in verse two makes it clear that we were all bound to the system of this word and therefore were slaves to "doing the desires of the flesh and of the mind."

No one is capable of breaking the power of sin without the grace of God being applied to his or her heart. This freedom from being a slave to trespassing against God is "not of yourselves, it is the gift of God; not of works, that no man should glory." Being made free from the grip of sin is truly a divine work in the heart and life of the Christian musician. From my personal experience I know that I was dead in trespasses and sins and that I only have forgiveness and freedom from the power of sin because of the unmerited favor of Christ Jesus. Therefore, I do not have anything to brag about when it comes to who I was when Christ found me under the bondage and load of sin. I have given up the sense of ownership of my life and my musicing because I am Christ's servant, and as a servant I have responsibilities rather than rights.

Song for the Day

I Believe in a Hill Called Mount Calvary by William J. Gaither, Gloria Gaither and Dale Oldham

Thought for the Day

"For by grace are ye saved through faith; and that not of yourselves: it is the gift of God: Not of works, lest any man should boast." (Ephesians 2:8-9)

July 2

Singing and Playing Under God's Wings

Psalm 63:7 — "Because thou hast been my help, therefore in the shadow of thy wings will I rejoice [*ranan*, 7442]."

Twenty-eight other times in the Old Testament, *ranan* was translated as some form of singing. Furthermore, the word *ranan* connotes not only singing but also emitting stridulous sound. The English word *stridulous* is an instrumental term for the sound that is produced when a string is played by a pick or a finger. So, it seems reasonable to believe that it is referring to singing and playing a stringed musical instrument in this verse.

The sweet psalmist of Israel declared that he was able to sing and play when he was under great stress. "It is most probable that the Psalm was written when David took refuge in the forest of Hareth, in the wilderness of Ziph, when he fled from the court of Achish."[1] This verse tells us that he was able to do so because, in his words, he was under the wings of *Elohim* the supreme God. The mental imagery that David used here is that God's wings were sufficient to give him solace, comfort and protection in the time of great trouble. God's wings proved to be big enough to give David shade and protection so that he could sing and play this wonderful psalm. If God's wings were big enough to protect David, they are big enough to take care of you and me when we are under great stress.

Scripture for the Day

Psalm 91:4 says, "He shall cover thee with his feathers, and under his wings shalt thou trust: his truth shall be thy shield and buckler."

Song for the Day

Under His Wings by William O. Cushing

Though for the Day

Only the Supreme God can make it possible for a Christian to sing and play with joy while going through a time of great stress.

July 3

Forgiving Your Brother

St. Luke 17:3-4 — "Take heed to yourselves: If thy brother trespass against thee, rebuke him; and if he repent, forgive him. And if he trespass against thee seven times in a day, and seven times in a day turn again to thee, saying, I repent; thou shalt forgive him."

Wow! The words of Jesus often trouble us, because most of us do not like conflict, so we fail to go to our brother directly and confront him (or her) when he or she trespasses (commits an offence) against us. It is much easier to do the wrong thing and go to someone else and talk to them about the offence against us than it is to go directly to the offender. Jesus said to rebuke (*epitimao* 2008) i.e., to censure or admonish the one who committed the offense.

If you think the first part of what Jesus said to do is difficult to understand, how about the second part? Jesus very succinctly stated, "Forgive him." When I read this the other day I decided to look up the word *aphiemi* (863) to make sure it meant forgive. Sure enough it means, let go, disregard, keep no longer, leave behind, and of course, forgive!

If you think the first and second parts of the admonishment that Jesus gave are hard to understand, how about the third part? Jesus told His disciples to keep on forgiving even after many offences.

Musicians are very emotional people. They get hurt very easily because they are sensitive people. It is no wonder that they get hurt when someone actually does something to them that is definitely wrong. However, it is never right to fester over something that someone else has done. You may be right about the situation, but if you do not forgive the offender you are in the wrong.

Song for the Day

All Your Anxiety by Edward H. Joy

Quote for the Day

My former pastor and great friend Rev. R. E. Carroll once told me, "Garen, when someone has committed a wrong against me, when I go to prayer I say to the Lord, 'Lord, handle me. Lord, will you please take care of my attitude.'"

Prayer for the Day

Dear Lord, I want You to give me a forgiving spirit. Help me to be able to forgive those who have committed an offence against me. Help me to forgive others even if they do not ask me to forgive them. Lord, You said in Your Word to forgive, so help me to be able to truly forgive. This petition I am praying in Your all-powerful and wise name. Amen.

July 4

Heeding the Trumpeter's Warning

Jeremiah 6:17 — "Also I set watchmen over you, saying, Hearken to the sound of the trumpet. But they said, We will not hearken."

God sets those over us who are able to watch over our souls. In this verse, Jeremiah refers to the sounding of the trumpet (*shofar* 7782) to warn the people of impending danger. The watchman entreated the people by saying, "Harken to the sound of the trumpet." All the people had to do was to listen to the trumpet and heed its warning. However, they made conscious choice not to pay attention to its warning sound.

What is your response to the warnings of "God's trumpeter?" Is His trumpeter sounding an alarm in your heart? Are you aware of something in your life that needs adjustment? Christian musicians need to remember that God sets the watchman in your path and causes His trumpeter to sound the alarm because He loves you and wants you to make it to heaven. The Israelites told the prophet, "we will not harken." God has placed watchmen over your life. His ministers and His Word are sounding His warnings as loving, caring acts of kindness toward you. He is a loving Father who cares for your soul. So, respond to the trumpeter's call.

Song for the Day

Guide Me O Thou Great Jehovah by Thomas Hastings

Thought for the Day

The shofar was an instrument of great strength. God had the watchman play it so that all could be warned in times of danger. The rebellious people did not take advantage of its warnings because they had purposed in their hearts not to listen.

Prayer for the Day

Lord, You are wonderful, merciful, wise and kind. I want to thank You for sending watchmen to care for my soul. Thank You for sending the blessed Holy Spirit to lead and guide me through this troubled world. Please give me the wisdom to listen to Your trumpeter's sound. Please help me to purpose in my heart to obey the checks of the Spirit. Help me to have a heart void of offence toward my God. Amen.

July 5

Understanding Worship

Exodus 34:14— "For thou shalt worship [*shachah* 7812] no other god: for the Lord, whose name is Jealous, is a jealous God."

Matthew 4:10— "Then saith Jesus unto him, Get thee hence, Satan: for it is written, Thou shalt worship [*proskuneo* 4352] the Lord thy God, and him only shalt thou serve."

Luke 4:8— "And Jesus answered and said unto him, Get thee behind me, Satan: for it is written, Thou shalt worship [*proskuneo*] the Lord thy God, and him only shalt thou serve."

The word *shachah* used in Exodus 34:14 means to prostrate oneself before God. Likewise the word *proskuneo* used in Matthew 4:10 and in St. Luke 4:8 means to prostrate oneself before God. This explanation of the nature of worship gives us the mental picture of worship as a posture and an attitude instead of an event to be consumed by a congregation for their personal enjoyment.

If the Bible definition of worship is prostrating oneself literally and figuratively before Almighty God, then what is the proper attitude for the Christian's musicing unto God in public worship? Most assuredly musical worship is not a public event where the church attender and participator use the God-created and God-given art of music to satiate his or her entertainment fancy.

Strong's Concordance defines *proskuneo* (4352) to "prostrate oneself in homage (do reverence to, adore):—worship." Certainly this definition of worship places a new light on worship for most of us. So much of public worship has grown to be about the individual who has come to the public worship service, that God often is forced, by our worship styles, to share His glory with us.

Song for the Day

Father I Adore You by Terry Coelho

Thought for the Day

My former pastor R.E. Carroll used to tell us that we should practice the presence of God every day of the week rather than only when we came to church to worship on Sunday.

Prayer for the Day

Dear Father in heaven, please forgive me for being so selfish in my attitudes of worship. Lord, I am often needy when I enter Your house. I do not mean to obscure Your glory with my troubles and needs, but I know that many times my mind is on my problems rather than Your glory. Please help me to come before Your presence with singing, rejoicing and an attitude of praise for who You are and what You have done. These things I am praying in Your name. Amen.

July 6

I Want to Be a Happy Musician

II Samuel 23:1-4 — "Now these be the last words of David. David the son of Jesse said, and the man who was raised up on high, the anointed of the God of Jacob, and the sweet psalmist of Israel, said, The Spirit of the LORD spake by me, and his word was in my tongue. The God of Israel said, the Rock of Israel spake to me, He that ruleth over men must be just, ruling in the fear of God. And he shall be as the light of the morning, when the sun riseth, even a morning without clouds; as the tender grass springing out of the earth by clear shining after rain."

It was Samuel (II Samuel 23:1-2) who called David the *naiym zamar* or "sweet psalmist" when he recorded the last words of David. When studying the meaning of the Hebrew words *naiym* (5273) *zamar* (2167) it becomes apparent that the term "sweet psalmist" mean that David was a musician who produced delightful or pleasant singing and playing, or at least we know from these words that his instrumental music was pleasant, and there is no reason to believe that his singing was not as pleasant as his playing.

As Christian musicians, our singing and playing should be pleasant. I am afraid that many Christian musicians are not very happy when they music unto God. It is a trick of Satan to cause Christian musicians to music in frustration and tension. The Bible says in Nehemiah 8:10, "… the joy of the LORD is your strength." It also says in Psalm 27:6, "And now shall mine head be lifted up above mine enemies round about me: therefore will I offer in his tabernacle sacrifices of joy; I will sing, yea, I will sing praises unto the LORD."

If Christians do not music with joy, their singing and playing will not be very sweet. I have purposed in my heart to be known as a musician who musics unto God with joy and sweetness like David, who was known as the "sweet psalmist of Israel."

Song for the Day

Majestic Sweetness by Samuel Stennett

Thought for the Day

Since the gospel message of our precious Lord and Savior Jesus Christ is good news, those of us who music unto Him should get a smile out of at least one side of our mouth when we sing unto Him.

Prayer for the Day

Dear heavenly Father, I believe that You can help me to be a happy musician. Please help me to music unto You with joy and gladness. Help me to love You so much that I will express my love through my musicing. Help me to be known as the musician who is a *"naiym zamar."* Give me more passion for You, so that that it will flow out of me when I music. These things I am praying in Your beautiful and wonderful name. Amen.

July 7

Desert Pete

Matthew 25:23 — "His lord said unto him, Well done, good and faithful servant; thou hast been faithful over a few things, I will make thee ruler over many things: enter thou into the joy of thy lord."

There is a secular country song written by Billy Ed Wheeler that has been a source of encouragement and inspiration to me over several years. I have shared its wisdom with the college students who have traveled with me on many spring tours. The song is about a man who was traveling through a desert. Exhausted and thirsty he sat down to rest, and to his surprise he saw a water pump.

The traveler looked at the pump in the distance and thought that he was seeing a mirage at first, but as he approached the old rusty pump, he realized that it was very real. He found a note that explained that there was a bottle of water under a rock that must be used to prime the pump.

This song is certainly not a "spiritual song" but it contains much wisdom about life that I have often applied to Christian musicians. The thirsty traveler had a choice to make. He could either drink the stale water in the jar or he could use it to prime the pump. The note went on to say, "Have faith my friend there's water down below… You've got to prime the pump; you must have faith and believe. You've got to give of yourself 'fore you're worthy to receive."

Wow, what wonderful wisdom desert Pete gave that may be applied to the lives and actions of Christian musicians. The world teaches musicians to "get all you can and can all you get." The musician who is sold out to Christ believes like Desert Pete that "You've got to give of yourself 'fore you're worthy to receive." So the Christian musician must believe that musicians should "Get all they can and give all they get to others."

Desert Pete gave one final instruction to the person who would read his note left in the baking powder can: "Drink all the water you can hold, wash your face and cool your feet. Leave the bottle full for others, thank you kindly, Desert Pete." I have often told the college students who were traveling with me on the "big bus," if you are going to feed others spiritually, you must eat, i.e., you must partake of the means of grace that God has provided for us all.

Every talented Christian musician must make the decision to consume musicing on his or her own desires or to pour out that musician's God-given talents in order to "prime the pump." If we give of ourselves, these musical offerings will help to sustain the spiritual life of others.

The thirsty, weary traveler gave this report: "So I poured

in the jar and I started pumpin' and I heard a beautiful sound of water bubblin' and splashin' up outta that hole in the ground. I took off my shoes and I drunk my fill of that cool, refreshing treat. I thank the Lord and thank the pump and I thank old Desert Pete."

As I mentioned earlier, this song is certainly not a "spiritual song" but it gives us much wisdom about life. If we, as Christian musicians, will not only utilize the means of grace to help to sustain our spiritual lives, but also leave "a bottle full for others," we can, like the weary traveler, give a good report when we have finished our journey. God sees when we first "prime the pump" and when we "leave a bottle full for others." We must remember that "You've got to give of yourself 'fore you're worthy to receive." If we remain good, unselfish and faithful we will hear our Lord say, "Well done, good and faithful servant; thou hast been faithful over a few things, I will make thee ruler over many things: enter thou into the joy of thy lord."

Song for the Day

Others by Charles D. Meigs

Thought for the Day

The decision to give and give and give of ourselves may seem foolish to many people but is often necessary if we are going to accomplish the task that is at hand.

July 8

Ministering by Accident

II Chronicles 29:25 — "And he set the Levites in the house of the LORD with cymbals, with psalteries, and with harps, according to the commandment of David, and of Gad the king's seer, and Nathan the prophet: for so was the commandment of the LORD..."

They included David the king, Gad the prophet or (seer), the venerated prophet Nathan, and YHVH Himself in their choices of church musicians. Think about it: all those austere bosses and God Himself were in on the selection of these ancient musicians to minister through music in the Temple. Surely no one could claim that these musicians were a part of Temple music ministry by accident.

Do you ever feel that you are ministering where you are now by a simple accident? Do you consider your music ministry a sacred trust? Do you really believe that God cares specifically about your music ministry? Do you believe that your music ministry is a part of God's wonderful plan for your life? Do you believe that God has placed you where you are ministering so that you will be able to touch people's lives spiritually? I have so much faith in our wonderful God that I believe with my whole heart that He has placed you there, because He has faith in you and believes that your music ministry is valuable to His great kingdom on this earth. I trust God on your behalf to help and guide you as you give this part of your life back to Him. So, your music ministry is worthwhile and God will make it efficacious if you will put it in His big wonderful, powerful and wise hands.

Song for the Day

Gentle Shepherd by Gloria and William Gaither.

Thought for the Day

It is one thing to say that you trust God, but it is entirely another to actually place your music ministry in His mighty hands and pray in belief that He will guide it every week.

Prayer for the Day

Our dear wonderful, kind, all-knowing heavenly Father, I am asking You to touch all those who have submitted their musical talent and their musical ministry to You. Lord, I am asking You to pour out a blessing on these who are truly Your ministering servants and undergird them with Your mighty hand. Lift them up in the most holy faith, so that they may truly be a blessing to those to whom they minister musically. These earnest petitions I bring to You. Amen.

July 9

The Learner is not Above the Teacher

Luke 6:40— "The disciple is not above his master: but every one that is perfect shall be as his master."

Adam Clarke had this to say about verse forty: "Everyone who is thoroughly instructed in Divine things, who has his heart united to God, whose disordered tempers and passions are purified and restored to harmony and order; everyone who has in him the mind that was in Christ, though he cannot be above, yet will be as, his teacher—holy, harmless, undefiled, and separate from sinners."[2]

Albert Barnes further explained, "The learner is not above his teacher, does not know more, and must expect to fare no better. This seems to have been spoken to show them that they were not to expect that their disciples would go beyond them in attainments; that if they were blind, their followers would be also; and that therefore it was important for them to understand fully the doctrines of the gospel, and not to be blind leaders of the blind."[3]

Matthew Poole had this to say on the statement, "…for the disciple is not above his master, none must look to learn of another more than the teacher knoweth himself. But it is better applied to Christ, and is as much as if our Lord had said, I am your Master, you are my disciples, and by that relation engaged to learn of me, and to follow me. I have taught you no more than I am ready to practice; I am merciful, I forgive, I give, looking for nothing again. I do not look that you should do anything above me, any thing as to which I have not set you, or shall not set you, an example; but your perfection lieth in coming as near to me as you can, in being as your Master."[4]

Every Christian musician should be a student of Christ's teachings. If he or she is, there will be a carefulness to impregnate these principles in that musician's musicing. Christ is not expecting great feats from us, but He is expecting us to be thoroughly taught. The word *katartizo* (2675) which is translated perfect in the AV means to be completely or thoroughly repaired or taught. Sometimes God has to repair or adjust our thinking. We must be willing to let Christ teach us, because we are not above our teacher.

Song for the Day

He Leadeth Me by Joseph H. Gilmore.

Thought for the Day

The word inspiration (*theopneustos* 2315) used in 2 Timothy 3:16 means "divinely breathed in." Therefore, it is of little wonder that theologians say that God cannot be separated from His Word.

Prayer for the Day

Our dear loving and all-wise heavenly Father, I am asking You to repair any false thinking that I may have about what You have taught us in Your Word. I am aware that I am hardheaded at times and am slow to learn new concepts about You. Lord, I confess that I need Your help. I know that the blessed Holy Spirit is the only completely safe teacher. So melt and mold my thinking until it is in agreement with Your truth which You have given us in Your inspired Word. These petitions I am praying in Your perfect name. Amen.

July 10

Blessed While Splitting Wood

Psalm 71:18 — "Now also when I am old and greyheaded, O God, forsake me not; until I have shewed thy strength unto this generation, and thy power to every one that is to come."

This morning I finished splitting wood that we will burn this winter. When I was folding the big splitting beam down to transport the splitter, I praised God for the gas operated splitter, the wood which had all been given to me, and for the strength that God had given me to do this kind of work.

I also thought about the Scripture in Psalm 37:25 that says, "I have been young, and now am old; yet have I not seen the righteous forsaken, nor his seed begging bread." A few days ago I realized that I did not have enough wood to make it through the winter. I breathed a short prayer to my heavenly Father and went on about my everyday chores. About two weeks ago the utility company started putting in some new electric poles on our street and wouldn't you know it, they had to cut some trees to get the job done. Hence, I received four loads of wood that need splitting. I do not know about you, but I believe that my God cares about my wood supply for this winter. I am grey headed and am of an age that somewhat qualifies me as being old. I received a blessing this morning when God brought these Scriptures to my remembrance.

You may not be grey headed and you may not need wood for this winter, but you do have needs and your heavenly Father cares about them. No matter how big or small they are, I am convinced that, as Philippians 4:19 promises, "… my God shall supply all your need according to his riches in glory by Christ Jesus."

Song for the Day

This is My Father's World by Maltbie D. Babcock

Thought for the Day

If a Christian does not recognize God's working in the little things in his or her life, he or she may not believe that God will work in the big things.

Prayer for the Day

I want to take time to thank You, Lord, for the reality of seeing You work on my behalf. Once again, I want to thank You for supplying a real need in my life according to Your riches in Christ Jesus. Thank You, Lord, for reminding me that You own all the trees on the street where I live. Thank You for being such a wonderful God. These thanks I now give, amen.

July 11

The Tongue of the Wise is Health

Proverbs 12:18-20 — "There is that speaketh like the piercings of a sword: but the tongue of the wise is health. The lip of truth shall be established for ever: but a lying tongue is but for a moment. Deceit is in the heart of them that imagine evil: but to the counsellors of peace is joy."

I learned a life lesson from a music colleague of mine who is now in heaven. Professor Archie Coons was a great Christian and a great music teacher. He and I had many conversations during the years that we worked together. There were some people whose offices I avoided when possible, because I always had enough problems that were capable of sending me to the slough of despond without hearing any more depressing news. However, it was different with Mr. Coons! He always had a smile on his face and an upbeat demeanor.

He had a lot of physical problems that were at times very serious, but he did not let them get him down emotionally. We would discuss all kinds of problems, but he never said anything demeaning or destructive about anyone. I always joked that if he saw two dead rats in the gutter, he would look them over and find something good to say about both of them. So the Scripture verses in Proverbs describes him as a person who had "the lip of truth." He was truly a counsellor of peace and joy. So, if you have the opportunity to say something negative and demeaning about someone today—don't do it.

Song for the Day

Since Jesus Came into My Heart by Rufus H. McDaniel

Prayer for the Day

Lord, You are a wonderful God. I want to thank You for giving me the opportunity to work with great Christian people. Thank You for the life lessons that I learn from them. Lord, help me to finish my days on this earth with a smile on my face and a joyful heart. Help me to continue to benefit from the lessons that I have learned and to mentor young musicians as positively as I have been mentored. Help me to not only music with joy, but to also live with "lips of truth" and a heart that is filled with words of peace and joy. Thank You that I can live a fruitful life and have a positive outlook. Amen.

July 12

Do You Feel Like Praising God?

Psalm 96:1-4— "O sing unto the LORD a new song: sing unto the LORD, all the earth. Sing unto the LORD, bless his name; shew forth his salvation from day to day. Declare his glory among the heathen, his wonders among all people. For the LORD is great, and greatly to be praised: he is to be feared above all gods."

Psalm18:3,6— "I will call upon the LORD, who is worthy to be praised: so shall I be saved from mine enemies… In my distress I called upon the LORD, and cried unto my God: he heard my voice out of his temple, and my cry came before him, even into his ears."

Are you catching on to the thought that I am emphasizing? If the past few days haven't been the most joyful and stress free, try blessing the LORD by singing "new song," i.e., a song of praise unto Him. You are probably thinking that you do not feel like singing or praising God at this time. I suggest that you do it anyway. What could it hurt? Perhaps you will find that obeying God's Word will be a help to your stressed condition.

You might even try telling someone who you work with who is not a Christian something God has done for you in the past. Something such as, "I thank God that He has given me a wonderful wife or I have been so blessed to grow up in such a wonderful family." Surely you can think of something good that the Lord has done for you. As the little chorus I once heard says, "It's amazing what praising can do."

Song for the Day

Let All the People Praise Thee by Lelia N. Norris

Thought for the Day

It is a truism that the Christian musicians who need to sing God's praises the most are those musicians who do not feel like singing or praising.

Prayer for the Day

Lord, You are a wonderful caring God who is concerned when Your musicians are depressed. Since You are a God who is above all gods, You are truly worthy to be praised even when I do not feel like praising, or singing for that matter. Lord, I love You and want You to know that I believe that You are able to lift me up from this pit of noise and depression. Thank You in advance for what You are going to do for me this day! This I am praying in Your trustworthy name. Amen.

July 13

Jesus Calls Us

Luke 9:23— "And he said to them all, If any man will come after me, let him deny himself, and take up his cross daily, and follow me."

I have been thinking about a great hymn for several days. One of my early memories of this hymn was hearing my pastor's wife, Mary Carroll, sing it as a call to worship from the place where she always sat on the left side of the sanctuary of our church in Merriam, Kansas. She had a beautiful voice that was easy to listen to in the context of Sunday morning worship. However, the thing that I remember the most was God's presence that settled over the worshipping body of believers that morning. There was simply no doubt about it, God was pleased with her sincere musical offering that Sunday morning. I have included the words of Cecil F. Alexander's hymn that she sang:

> Jesus calls us o'er the tumult
> Of our life's wild, restless, sea;
> Day by day His sweet voice soundeth,
> Saying, "Christian, follow Me!"

> Jesus calls us from the worship
> Of the vain world's golden store,
> From each idol that would keep us,
> Saying, "Christian, love Me more!"

In our joys and in our sorrows,
Days of toil and hours of ease,
Still He calls, in cares and pleasures,
"Christian, love Me more than these!"

Jesus calls us! By Thy mercies,
Savior, may we hear Thy call,
Give our hearts to Thine obedience,
Serve and love Thee best of all.

—CECIL FRANCES ALEXANDER (1852)

Thought for the Day

Although Christian musicians may deny it, they sometimes pick up some figurative idols along life's way that are doubtlessly a hindrance to true worship.

Prayer for the Day

I want to Thank You, Jesus, for faithfully calling us to love You more. Lord, please help me to not put anything in the way of my worshipping You. Please help me to hear Your call in both times of joy and sorrow. As the song teaches, help me to give my heart to fully obeying Your will. This I pray in Your merciful and wise name. Amen.

July 14

Publish the Gospel with Great Joy

Jeremiah 31:7— "For thus saith the LORD; Sing with gladness [*simchah*] for Jacob, and shout [*tsahal*] among the chief of the nations: publish [*shama*] ye, praise ye, and say, O LORD, save thy people, the remnant of Israel.

Strong believed that the Hebrew word *shama* (8085) was a primitive root which meant to hear intelligently. Thus it is safe to deduce that this word means to publish God's message in such a way that people will be able to discern or understand its meaning.

The musicians in ancient Israel were instructed to "sing with gladness." The word *simchah* (8057) connotes much more than our English word gladness does. *Simchah* meant with exceeding gladness or blithesomeness. If it was necessary for these ancient musicians to sing God's message with such extreme joy that included *tsahal* (6670), i.e., shouting, then we should take notice that we should music unto God with extreme joy. So, do not let anyone convince you that our musicing unto God should be sedate and blasé. On the contrary, praise to God should be a great shout of acclamation that flows from a musician with a holy heart-life.

This verse of Scripture in Jeremiah 31:7 states, "For thus saith the Lord; Sing with gladness..." Do you sing with great gladness? Is your heart full of joy and adoration toward God? I have always told vocalists who studied with me that any musician whose heart is bursting with joy and thanksgiving on the inside will not be able to look like the great stone face when he or she sings unto the Lord. If you have real, genuine, authentic joy on the inside it will get out when you music unto God. So, do not try to hold your joy on the inside. Be as emotional about the good news of the gospel as you are about your favourite sports team winning a game.

Song for the Day

Holy Spirit be My Guide by Mildred Cope

Thought for the Day

The only church musicians that do not have a right to music unto God with great joy are those who try to sing about Him without knowing Him personally.

Quote for the Day

"We make a vast mistake if we think that the Holy Spirit's work is limited only to salvation."[5]

Prayer for the Day

Lord, I am convicted about my musicing unto You. Lord, You know that from the bottom of my heart and soul I want to music unto You with great passion! I am asking at the beginning of this day to help me to sing unto Your great and mighty name with the *dunamis* of the Holy Spirit. I am asking in the most earnest way to help me to live a life in the Holy Spirit so that Your love and power will flow out of my inner-most being when I sing or lead others in singing unto You. Amen.

July 15

We Must Worship the Creator (Part 1)

Romans 1:25 — "Who changed the truth of God into a lie, and worshipped and served the creature more than the Creator, who is blessed for ever. Amen."

What is worship all about? Because of the reality of God's presence in our lives, we worship! We worship God for who He is, what He has done, and what He is presently doing now in our lives. We pray, we read Scripture, we preach the Word, we confess His name, and we also music unto Him.

We worship the Creator, not the created things. Romans 1:25 tells us about what happened to those who worship created things rather than the one who created all things. They historically had been those "Who changed the truth of God into a lie, and worshipped and served the creature [i.e., the created] more [rather] than the Creator, who is blessed for ever." Music is a created thing. It is dangerous to worship music. As a matter of fact, it is idolatrous to worship music. Worshipping musical performance is the result of a fundamental misunderstanding of the purpose of Church music in worship. The listener-performer phenomenon is a misuse of music in worship.

Song for the Day

O Worship the King by Sir Robert Grant

Thought for the Day

If our musicing is not solidly placed under the lordship of Christ, there is a danger that it will give glory to someone other than Him.

July 16

We Must Worship the Creator (Part 2)

Psalm 68:4 — "Sing unto God, sing praises to his name: extol him that rideth upon the heavens by his name JAH, and rejoice before him."

Have you ever pondered on the thought of why we include music in our public and private worship of God? Why don't we just speak all our worship to God? Why do we music unto Him? Musicing unto God helps us to understand and express effectively who God is and what He does. In the act of musicing we are able to express our response to the claims of God upon our lives. Sometimes words alone cannot fully express the depth of our response to God; so, we music unto Him.

Genesis 1:1 states that "In the beginning God created the heaven and the earth." Colossians 1:16 tells us, "For by him were all things created, that are in heaven, and that are in earth, visible and invisible, whether they be thrones, or dominions, or principalities, or powers: all things were created by him, and for him." Hebrews 2:10-

12 further explains why we music unto God when it says,

"For it became him, for whom are all things, and by whom are all things, in bringing many sons unto glory, to make the captain of their salvation perfect through sufferings. For both he that sanctifieth and they who are sanctified are all of one: for which cause he is not ashamed to call them brethren, Saying, I will declare thy name unto my brethren, in the midst of the church will I sing praise unto thee."

Verses 16-18 continues,

"For verily he took not on him the nature of angels; but he took on him the seed of Abraham. Wherefore in all things it behoved him to be made like unto his brethren, that he might be a merciful and faithful high priest in things pertaining to God, to make reconciliation for the sins of the people. For in that he himself hath suffered being tempted, he is able to succour them that are tempted."

Hebrews 4:14-16 caps it all off with these words,

"Seeing then that we have a great high priest, that is passed into the heavens, Jesus the Son of God, let us hold fast our profession. For we have not an high priest which cannot be touched with the feeling of our infirmities; but was in all points tempted like as we are, yet without sin. Let us therefore come boldly unto the throne of grace, that we may obtain mercy, and find grace to help in time of need."

Thought for the Day

Christian musicians should not have any trouble worshipping the Creator of music rather than worshipping the music itself because God is worthy of our worship.

July 17

We Must Worship the Creator (Part 3)

Psalm 47:5-7— "God is gone up with a shout, the LORD with the sound of a trumpet. Sing praises to God, sing praises: sing praises unto our King, sing praises. For God is the King of all the earth: sing ye praises with understanding."

The worshipper must know, i.e., understand (Psalm 47:7), the fundamental truths about God and His nature before musical worship can be authentic or real. Furthermore, the worshipper must be living in fellowship and relationship with God before musical worship can be authentic and real. I have often said that it is one thing to know about God, but it is completely another to actually know God. The musician who does not know God, by having a personal relationship with Him, cannot sing from first-hand experience.

Jesus told the Samaritan woman that "Ye worship ye know not what." Jesus said in St. John 4:24, "God is a Spirit: and they that worship him must worship him in spirit and in truth." Paul told the Corinthian church in I Corinthians 14:15b, "I will sing with the spirit [4151 *pneuma* - spirit, Holy Spirit], and I will sing with the understanding also." The Greek word *nous* (3563) translated intellect here, means to sing with the Christian musician's intellect, i.e. mind.

Also, Psalm 47:6-7 states, "Sing praises to God, sing praises: sing praises unto our King, sing praises. For God is the King of all the earth: sing ye praises with understanding." The Hebrew word *sakal* (7919) translated understanding means that the musician must be circumspect and must walk with prudence, skill and wisdom. This word also connotes that a Christian musician must sing with intelligence.

Thought for the Day

There would be much less trouble with church music if church musicians would spend as much time learning to know God as they do learning their music.

July 18

How to Become an Unashamed Christian Musician

1 John 4:17-18— "Herein is our love made perfect, that we may have boldness in the day of judgment: because as he is, so are we in this world. There is no fear in love; but perfect love casteth out fear: because fear hath torment. He that feareth is not made perfect in love."

As a Christian musician you may be wondering how it is possible that you could possibly stand at the day of judgment without fear. 1 Peter 1:13-16 gives some brief instruction in what the Christian can do to make this possible. "Wherefore gird up the loins of your mind, be sober, and hope to the end for the grace that is to be brought unto you at the revelation of Jesus Christ; As obedient children, not fashioning yourselves according to the former lusts in your ignorance: But as he which hath called you is holy, so be ye holy in all manner of conversation; Because it is written, Be ye holy; for I am holy."

Romans 5:5 explains that God makes this hope possible when it states, "And hope maketh not ashamed; because the love of God is shed abroad in our hearts by the Holy Ghost which is given unto us." However, it is our responsibility to take control of our thought life. St. Paul declared in Ephesians 6:14-17, "Stand therefore, having your loins girt about with truth, and having on the breastplate of righteousness; And your feet shod with the preparation of the gospel of peace; Above all, taking the shield of faith, wherewith ye shall be able to quench all the fiery darts of the wicked. And take the helmet of salvation, and the sword of the Spirit, which is the word of God."

So, there are several things that the Christian musician needs to do to become an unashamed Christian. We do not have to live a defeated Christian life. It is a mistake to take the "poor pitiful me" defeatist attitude about Christian living. God wants us to be proactive Christians. He wants to guard our hearts and minds. So, do not listen to Satan or Christians who will whisper in your ear that you cannot live a victorious Christ-like life.

Song for the Day

Victory in Jesus by Eugene M. Bartlett

Thought for the Day

The Children of Israel wondered around in the wilderness for forty years, but that wouldn't have been necessary if they had listened to God. I know He knew the way through the wilderness, but He also knew the way around the wilderness.

July 19

A Good Thing to Confess

Psalm 92:1-2— "It is a good thing to give thanks unto the LORD, and to sing praises unto thy name, O Most High: To shew forth thy lovingkindness in the morning, and thy faithfulness every night..."

The superscription of this psalm identifies it as "A Psalm or Song for the Sabbath Day." It is a wonderful creedal confession. We as Christian musicians should often confess to the independent, self-existent eternal God that it is a good thing to give thanks (*yada* 3034) i.e. to hold out our hands in avowal to God. Christian musicians should be quick to raise our hands before God as an expression of honor to our precious Lord and Savior.

These verses are also a confession that is a good thing to sing praises unto our God. The words "sing praises" have been translated from the Hebrew word *zamar* (2167). Thus we confess that it is a good thing to play the strings of a musical instrument as we sing unto our God.

Christian musician, do not ever let Satan convince you that your musicing unto God is a waste of time. The effectual fervent musicing of a righteous musician can avail much! Satan knows that he cannot get you to rob a bank or steal a car, but if you are not careful, he might get you to "sit in the seat of the scornful" (Psalm 1:1). If he can get you to become depressed, then he can cause your musical ministry to become ineffective. You must remember that the "joy of the LORD" is a musician's strength (Nehemiah 8:10).

You must take courage, Christian musician. Tell Satan, "In the name of Jesus Christ, get thee behind me, Satan!" We should remember the words of Martin Luther who wrote in the hymn "A Mighty Fortress" concerning Satan, that "One little word will fell him." That word will come from our advocate Jesus Christ the righteous one!

Song for the Day

A Mighty Fortress by Martin Luther

Thought for the Day

Since Satan is absolutely no match for God, Christian musicians should rely on God to take care of troubling situations that Satan has caused to arise in the place where we minister musically.

July 20

My Servants Sing for Joy

Isaiah 65:14– "Behold, my servants shall sing for joy of heart, but ye shall cry for sorrow of heart, and shall howl for vexation of spirit."

Today's discussion should cheer you with the promise in Isaiah that "My servants shall sing for joy of heart." If you are God's musical servant, this is a very precious promise for you. Christian musicians who live a life of musical servanthood have the right to sing unto God with great joy. True servants of God all may music with real joy which the prophet Isaiah called "joy of heart." True joy of heart is one of life's greatest blessings.

No one may notice that you are living a life of musical servanthood, but God sees everything you do for his kingdom. Jesus sees your good musical works that glorify your heavenly Father which is in heaven. No one else may, but God keeps accurate records. He, who sees your good works done quietly in His name, will reward you openly. Never forget that you are laying up treasures in heaven where nothing corrupts or can steal your heavenly treasure (Matthew 6:19).

You should be encouraged! You have the right to music, so exercise that right and "sing for joy." Make your boast in the Lord (Psalm 34:2). Continue with great joy to honor the Trinity with your musical offerings. Lift up God's name in the congregation of His people. Without reserve or shame let the whole world know that the LORD is the only true God who is alive and worthy to be worshipped. Music in God's name to all those you have the opportunity, that God is good! You should never, never, never, never quit ministering unto your heavenly Father, with great joy, as long as you have breath.

Thought for the Day

Musicians who are the musical servants of God never have to act like it is a joy to minister unto God, because they have the "joy of the Lord" in their hearts.

July 21

The Choice of Sorrow or Joy of Heart

Isaiah 65:14– "Behold, my servants shall sing for joy of heart, but ye shall cry for sorrow of heart, and shall howl for vexation of spirit."

This Scripture speaks of the rejection of those who had forsaken YHVH. God had called after them, but they had refused to respond to His admonition. We are often led to believe by the world that a sinful lifestyle brings happiness. The billboards and magazine ads show a false view of a "happy sinner." We never get a glimpse of the crying and sorrowfulness of heart of those who reject God and live a sinful life.

This Scripture shows an accurate picture of the righteous and the ungodly. The inspired prophet Isaiah boldly explained some of the results of both holy and unrighteous living. He stated that the righteous would sing for joy because of the inner peace in his or her heart, and that the ungodly would howl for sorrow of heart. The prophet's writing is not a novel idea since the Psalmist stated in the first Psalm that the godly would be blessed and that the ungodly would be like "…chaff which the wind driveth away."

Jesus said, as recorded in St. John 7:38, "He that believeth on me, as the Scripture hath said [Zechariah 14:8], out of his belly shall flow rivers of living water." It is no wonder that this blessed musician sings for joy of heart. The reason that the wicked musicians "howl" is that corruption, sorrow, vexation of spirit and sadness flow out of the life of the wicked. The reason that the righteous musicians are blessed and "sing for joy of heart" is that they have an inner peace that flows out of a holy heart life, so much so, that they have an outer joy when they music unto God.

So, cheer up musical servants of the Most High God, and sing and play with true joy of heart. Sing for joy because you are spiritually whole, truly happy and are free from the fractured dreams that come at the end of the ephemeral pleasures of a sinful life.

Prayer for the Day

LORD, thank You for a pure heart that can sing for joy. I can sing at the end of the day because You live in my heart. Please help me to always hear Your voice and be quick to respond to Your admonitions. Thank You for the rivers of living water that flow from a heart of love for You. I bless Your name this day because You have made me truly glad. I thank You, Lord, for Your love and gracious mercy to me. Amen.

July 22

Sow in Tears and Reap with Singing

Psalm 126:5-6 — "They that sow in tears shall reap in joy. He that goeth forth and weepeth, bearing precious seed, shall doubtless come again with rejoicing, bringing his sheaves with him."

The Hebrew word rendered joy in verse five and rejoicing in verse six is *rinnah* (7440) which means joy or singing or perhaps joy of singing. So we deduce from this word that weeping Christians are also singing Christians. Musicians, who go out weeping as they sow precious musical seed, will doubtless return singing and rejoicing.

Today I may feel like a musical failure and be tempted to turn in my resignation. However, I know better than to quit when I am very weary and depressed. As I read God's Word,

I re-read verses five and six of Psalm 126 and these verses give me the courage to believe that my musical ministry is worth every minute I spend.

Weeping over my musicing prepares my heart as a Christian musician, so that I may bear precious seed. I am realizing all over again that it is my job, as a Christian music director, to "go" and to "weep" and to "bear precious seed," and it is God's responsibility to "break the loaves and the fish" and to feed these the people's hearts of those to whom I am ministering. The proper musical attitude for me as a music minister is to music in a spirit of humility. If I do, God has promised to give me sheaves of harvest to bring, as a musical offering, to my heavenly father.

Song for the Day

A Charge To Keep I Have by Charles Wesley

Thought for the Day

God has promised to bless the Christian musician's musical ministry, if he or she will minister with the spirit of humility and tears of burden for those to whom we minister.

July 23

And Can It Be?

Romans 6:23— "For the wages of sin is death; but the gift of God is eternal life through Jesus Christ our Lord."

I am amazed that the mighty love of God reached a farm boy in Eastern Kansas. I know that the wages of sin is death. I understand that the law and justice of God demands penalty for sin. Even when I was a bitter young man that did not love and serve Jesus Christ, I never doubted the existence of God or that I would have to someday pay for my sin. I never doubted that God knew and saw my rebellion against Him.

In those rebellious years, I understood God to be stern more than loving. I did not understand the infinite grace of God that sent His Son to die for me. I did not fully understand that Christ "emptied Himself of all but love." It still amazes me that "He left His Father's throne above, so free, so infinite His grace!"

"And can it be that I should gain an interest in the Savior's blood?" Charles Wesley explained my sinful depraved condition very well when he wrote, "Long my imprisoned spirit lay, fast bound in sin and nature's night." However, praise be to God, "Thine eye diffused a quickening ray, I woke; the dungeon flamed with light! My chains fell off; my heart was free. I rose, went forth and followed Thee."

Wesley caught the reality of the born-again experience when he penned the words, "No condemnation now I dread; Jesus, and all in Him, is mine! Alive in Him, my living Head, and clothed in righteousness divine. Bold I approach the eternal throne and claim the crown, through Christ, my own." Praise God for His love that made it possible to be forgiven and set free from a life of rebellion and sin.

Song for the Day

And Can it Be? by Charles Wesley

Prayer for the Day

My dear Heavenly Father, I want to thank You for sending Your Son Jesus Christ into this sin-cursed world to die and pay the penalty for my sins. Thank You that Christ emptied Himself of all but love for me. Thank You that instead of wrath, I received mercy. Thank You for Your amazing love that reached a sinner like me. Amen.

July 24

God Never Gets Tired (Part 1)

Isaiah 40:28 — "Hast thou not known? hast thou not heard, that the everlasting God, the Lord, the Creator of the ends of the earth, fainteth not, neither is weary? there is no searching of his understanding."

The passage of Scripture in which this verse is found reminds the Christian that the LORD, who is the creator of everything above, below, in, on and around the earth, gives strength and power to the weary. God means what He said in the Book of Genesis. He really did create everything. (If one doubts the authenticity of God's literal creation in the Genesis record, he or she "dumbs down" the power of God.) If God did not create everything then perhaps He does not have the power and the ability to give strength to weary Christian musicians. I choose to believe, however, that Jehovah had the power to take nothing and make something out of that "nothingness;" and furthermore that Elohiym, who is still the supreme God, now has the power to give strength to weary Christian musicians.

I also choose to believe that God exercises that power on the behalf of weary Christian musicians. The reason I believe that God gives strength to weary Christian musicians is that I have experienced that power and strength many, many times since I confessed my sins with godly sorrow and received His forgiveness and, by faith, accepted Him as my Lord and Savior.

How can a weary Christian musician receive help and strength? The answer is very simple. It is so simple that many Christian musicians fail to receive this help and assistance from the self-existent, independent, eternal "God who is." First of all, musicians must remember that He is, and that He is the rewarder of them that seek Him. (See Hebrews 11:6.)

The same passage of Scripture that we quoted at the beginning of this discussion also says in verse 31, "But they that wait upon the LORD shall renew their strength; they shall mount up with wings as eagles; they shall run, and not be weary; they shall walk and not faint." The Hebrew word which has been translated renew in verse thirty-one is *caliph* (2498) which means literally a change in strength. So, if we as Christian musicians need to have a change in the amount of strength that we have, either physically, spiritually or emotionally, we need to "wait" (*qavah* 6960) or be "bound together" with the self-existent, independent, eternal God who is alive and seated at the right hand of the Father making intercession for Christian musicians right now! (See Romans 8: 26-27.) So, the secret of your renewed strength is getting close to the Lord and telling Him how much you need Him.

Quote for the Day

"I will lift up mine eyes unto the hills, from whence cometh my help. My help cometh from the LORD, which made heaven and earth." (Psalm 121:1-2.)

July 25

God Never Gets Tired (Part 2)

Isaiah 40:29 — "He giveth power to the faint; and to them that have no might he increaseth strength."

One of Satan's tricks is to get musicians so busy that they fail to wait upon God. The closer that a Christian musician is to God, the harder it becomes for Satan to tempt and to overcome that musician. Many times a Christian will find himself or herself in need of increased strength. Sometimes musicians need what I call a "spiritual oil change." In other words, we need to be freshly bound together with God.

One of the things that auto mechanics stress is that the moving parts of an engine need to have fresh oil that will stick to the cylinder walls, pistons and bearings. Without the freshness of clean oil, dirt and sludge will tend to gum up our spiritual engine. The fact that you had a fresh anointing from the blessed Holy Spirit a few months ago does not preclude the need for the fresh oil of the Spirit today. Again, auto mechanics tell us that you do not have to do anything wrong for your engine to be in need of an oil change. As a matter of fact, all you have to do is use that engine and it will routinely be in need of fresh oil.

Musicians who "wait upon the LORD" will have the fresh oil of the Spirit which is absolutely necessary to have the power to get above the troubles and temptations of Satan in this life. It is only by having the fresh oil (anointing) of the Holy Spirit that a Christian musician will be able to walk and run with spiritual power. Without this *dunamis* of the Spirit, the musician will become so spiritually weak that he or she will be in danger of failing.

The formula for receiving spiritual strength is simple. First, receive strength from God by believing that He is the creator of all things (including music). Second, believe that He created you personally, and therefore you belong to Him. Third, believe that He cares for all His creation, including you. Fourth, take time to be holy. Make sure that you spend time bringing yourself together with God. Fifth, lift up your heart and mind as though they were the wings of an eagle. And let God take you above and beyond your troubles. Sixth, receive strength from God to walk and run the spiritual race that has been set before you.

Prayer for the Day

Thank You, Lord, that You not only created worlds, but you have also created me. Thank You for caring enough about me to provide the means of grace that makes it possible for me to run this spiritual race. Thank You for Your Word that is steadfast and sure. Lord, I feel right now that I am spiritually faint, and that I need strength that only can come from You. I am asking You to please give me the strength necessary to music unto You. I know that I can trust You because You never faint or are weary. Amen.

July 26

Succeeding in Heaven's Eyes

Matthew 19: 29-30 — "And every one that hath forsaken houses, or brethren, or sisters, or father, or mother, or wife, or children, or lands, for my name's sake, shall receive an hundredfold, and shall inherit everlasting life. But many that are first shall be last; and the last shall be first." (Also read Mark 10:28-31 and Luke 13: 24-30.)

The verses above are powerful and even shocking examples of what Jesus Christ considered most important in this life. He very carefully said that if we want to be sent forth for Christ and His kingdom and inherit everlasting life, we will need to give up the sense of ownership of our families and possessions.

Those who love us the most often do not remember Christ's words to those of us who minister for Him. They want the very best for us. As a matter of fact they want us to be "first." Why? Because they believe with all their hearts that we "deserve it."

Christ gives this paradoxical statement in verse thirty "But many that are first shall be last; and the last shall be first." No one that loves us will want us to be last. Those who understand Christian work know that if we serve Christ out there in Smirgley Junction, we will be hidden away and will certainly be last. They know that we will come and go in this life without much earthly recognition or remuneration.

Our family and close friends will not always understand Christ's promise in Matthew 20:16, "So the last shall be first, and the first last: for many be called, but few chosen." Remember that in St. Matthew 19:29, Christ stated that those who forsake "for my name's sake shall receive an hundredfold..." And, of course, everlasting life. Christ sums it up very clearly in Matthew 20:28 — "Even as the Son of man came not to be ministered unto, but to minister, and to give His life a ransom for many."

Song for the Day

Jesus is All I Need by J. Rowe

Thought for the Day

Everything good that we have in this life is a gift from God.

Prayer for the Day

Lord, please forgive me for ever thinking about living the good life. Forgive me for thinking about "getting all I can and canning all I get." Help me to be a giver. Let me pour out my life for You. Help me to be "ready to go or ready to stay." Lord, I want to serve You. If I know my heart, I want to minister to others. Please let me live my life as a willing sacrifice to You. Thank You, Lord, for giving me the privilege to minister to those around me. Amen.

July 27

Seeking God

I Chronicles 16: 9-10 — "Sing unto him, sing psalms unto him, talk ye of all his wondrous works. Glory ye in his holy name: let the heart of them rejoice that seek the Lord."

As ministers of music we need to take heed of the wonderful formula laid down for the seeker after God. First, sing unto the Lord. Second, sing Psalms (*zamar 2167*), sing and play instruments unto the Lord. Third, talk about what the Lord has done. Fourth, glory (*halal 1984*) or boast about His holy name. Fifth, rejoice (*samach 8055*), be cheerful and glad and be of a merry heart as you seek the self-existent, eternal God who is.

Wow! What wonderful guidelines for those who seek after God. We, as ministers of music, should by our musicing foster an attitude of great joy for the God seeker. Evangelistic singing should be joyful singing. Nothing is said about sadness, groaning or depression. The Word says that the seeker should brighten up and be gleesome. God wants the seeker to cheer up. Why? Because the "good news" is the best news the seeker will ever hear in this life. The seeker after God should "Let the heart of them rejoice that seek the Lord." No long face, no despair, no doubt and no sad song is recommended. Be sure that you present the good news as good news— never sad or bad news!

Musicians have the wonderful privilege to help set an atmosphere conducive to seeking after God. Some seekers will not even know much about God. Many seekers will have a wrong concept of who God is and what He does for those who truly seek Him.

We as Christian musicians need to remember that we should also be seekers after God. Our musicing should be unto Him. As the verses in I Chronicles 16:9-10 tell us, we need to talk or sing of all His wondrous works. We need to be sure that as we music we "glory in His holy name." The same music that edifies the believers we minister to will also strengthen us spiritually if we let it draw us closer to the object of our worship, Jesus our great Savior.

Song for the Day

His Eye is on the Sparrow by C.D. Martin

Thought for the Day

Musician, do you really worship as you sing, play or direct music? Do you rejoice in the Lord as you music? The Scripture in I Chronicles admonishes us to rejoice as we seek the Lord.

Prayer for the Day

Thank You, Lord, for letting me sing the good news of Your saving and sanctifying power. Thank You that You do not require sad songs but rather glad songs. Lord ,help me to shine and make my boast in the Lord (Psalm 34:2). Please shine through me and flow through me. Help my musicing "show forth Thy glory."

July 28

Lifting up Your Voice Like a Trumpet

Isaiah 58:1— "Cry aloud, spare not, lift up thy voice like a trumpet, and shew my people their transgression, and the house of Jacob their sins."

The prophet Isaiah had a big job to do! The Jewish nation had fallen into idolatry. Their sin was great and they were very needy spiritually. Sounds like today, doesn't it? As a Christian musician you will have opportunities to minister to needy people. It will not be easy to take the time to minister to the musicians who you come into contact with. Church musicians and private music lesson teachers are busy people. Do not let yourself get so preoccupied with the music part of music ministry that you forget to reach out to those you minister to and to those on your own ministry team.

In order to be able to help others you must be in regular communication with God the source of real help. If you are going to feed others you must first be fed. If you are going to lift up your voice "like a trumpet" you must be on top spiritually.

This Scripture states that we are to show people their sins and transgressions. Wow! I don't know any music minister that enjoys pointing out others' sins. If we are not careful we will go through life sort of doing God's work while we miss the real point of being His ministering servants. If those whom we come in contact with continue in sin and miss heaven, we have failed them no matter how much music we teach them. We must remember that they will not make it to heaven if they continue sinning or have unconfessed sin in their lives.

The real importance of sacred musicing is that it is a ministering tool and a worship tool. The music part of music is very important, but it is not the main thing. Getting ready for heaven is the main thing. The most important thing to remember about church music is that it is a means of grace.

Song for the Day

Take Time To Be Holy by W.D. Longstaff

Thought for the Day

You cannot continually feed other people's souls unless you feed your own.

Prayer for the Day

Thank You, Lord, for music. Thank You, Lord, that You make it possible for me to draw closer to You through this wonderful means of grace. Please help me to remember that music is not the end of worship but an aid to worship. Help me to help others to prepare their hearts for worship and to regularly worship God through their musicing. Please anoint my musicing so that it may be a tool for the Holy Spirit to use to draw sinners to Christ.

July 29

Grace from the Lord Jesus Christ

1 Corinthians 1:3 — "Grace be unto you, and peace, from God our Father, and from the Lord Jesus Christ."

This was St. Paul's prayer for the Christians at Corinth. I am so grateful that I have personally received God's grace, mercy and peace instead of His justice. I tremble when I think about where I would be today if I had not received God's mercy and love. St. Paul reminded the saints at Corinth about the peace that ensues when one is a recipient of the grace of God through our Lord and Savior Jesus Christ.

In 1 Corinthians 1:4-8 St. Paul states,

"I thank my God always on your behalf, for the grace of God which is given you by Jesus Christ; That in every thing ye are enriched by him, in all utterance, and in all knowledge; Even as the testimony of Christ was confirmed in you: So that ye come behind in no gift; waiting for the coming of our Lord Jesus Christ: Who shall also confirm you unto the end, that ye may be blameless in the day of our Lord Jesus Christ."

Paul reminded them that those who were recipients of God's grace were enriched in utterance, knowledge and gifts, and that Christ's testimony was attested to by their Godly lives. The most precious thing that Paul said was that they were confirmed blameless in the sight of Jesus Christ our Lord and Savior.

St. Paul prayed for them, but Jesus is at this moment sitting at the right hand of God the Father praying for you and me, as Romans 8:34 attests, "Who is he that condemneth? It is Christ that died, yea rather, that is risen again, who is even at the right hand of God, who also maketh intercession for us." With this in mind, every ministering musician should rejoice in the truth that Christ the righteous judge is our advocate before the throne of God at this very minute.

Song for the Day

God's Great Grace by Floyd W. Hawkins

Thought for the Day

It is the truth that God's grace is amazing. It is the truth also that none of us will make it into the City of God without God's grace.

July 30

Jesus Expects Our Help

Mark 6:37— "He [Jesus] answered and said unto them [His disciples], give ye them to eat..."

After Jesus taught the people, his disciples wanted Jesus to send those He had taught away so they could go somewhere and buy something to eat. The disciples were overwhelmed at the enormous task of feeding 5,000 people. The job was too costly and too big for them, but it was not too big for Jesus.

Christian musicians are often just as overwhelmed at the tasks before them. Eighty thousand dollars for a new organ, seventy-nine thousand dollars for a new piano, two Sunday morning worship services, an adult choir, a youth choir, a children's choir, an Easter pageant, and a Christmas production with a special choir, orchestra, sets, lights and drama are definitely too much pressure and too taxing.

It often seems that Jesus is saying "do it all yourself." What we often forget is that He does expect our meager "five loaves and two fish," but when we present them to Jesus, He blesses our work and He provides for the five thousand. Jesus takes whatever we have and when He has blessed it, it is enough and will be sufficient to accomplish the ministry task.

It is our job to give of our best to the Master, and it is His job to bless our musical ministry so that it will be efficacious. Jesus did say that it is our responsibility to feed the souls of those who attend our worship services. However, He does not expect us to do it with our own strength or power. We are required to give Jesus all that we have, but we must remember that our musicing will accomplish the desired task if we will let him bless, break and feed it to all those who attend our worship services.

Song for the Day

Take My Life and Let it Be by F.R. Havergal

Thought for the Day

Jesus will never ask more than you are capable of giving.

Prayer for the Day

I am asking You, Lord, to forgive me for misunderstanding You and trying to do Your work in my own strength. I need and want Your help. Here is my musical lunch. It is meager, but it is all Yours. Please break it, bless it and feed the hungry multitude. This I pray in Your strong name. Amen.

July 31

Lean not unto Your own Understanding

Proverbs 3:5-6 — "Trust in the LORD with all thine heart; and lean not unto thine own understanding. In all thy ways acknowledge him, and he shall direct thy paths."

The word *batach* (982), which has been translated here as trust, means to go quickly to YHVH, the self-existent, independent, eternal God who is. Furthermore, this passage of scripture teaches that this trust must be complete and from the center of one's intellect. Verse six states, "In all thy ways acknowledge him, and he shall direct thy paths." The English word acknowledge (*yada* 3045) is used in a host of applications in the Bible and connotes having regard and respect for God. Because YHVH "is," rather than merely "was," He has the power and wisdom to direct the Christian musician's paths. Solomon, who was great and very wise, admonishes us to "lean not unto thine own understanding." Because YHVH is eternal and self-existent, He understands every path that a musician takes in his or her journey of obedience to Him.

Solomon went on to say in verses seven and eight, "Be not wise in thine own eyes: fear the LORD, and depart from evil. It shall be health to thy navel, and marrow to thy bones." Jesus said in Luke 10:21, "I thank thee, O Father, Lord of heaven and earth, that thou hast hid these things from the wise and prudent, and hast revealed them unto babes..." Spiritual knowledge and direction comes from God rather than from human wisdom. So, Solomon gave us good advice when he said that we should lean on the wisdom of the LORD rather than trusting our own understanding.

Song for the Day

Trust and Obey by John H. Sammis

Prayer for the Day

I want to thank You, LORD, that You have promised to provide us with understanding. You have also promised to direct our paths. So, please give me the good sense to do the leaning and let You do the guiding. Your word has promised that if I will trust Your wisdom that "It shall be health to thy navel, and marrow to thy bones." I am asking You to help me to lean on You and trust Your wisdom with my whole heart. This I am asking in Your all-wise and wonderful name. Amen.

Endnotes

2. Adam Clarke, *Job-Song of Solomon*. Vol. 3 in *Clarke's Commentary*, (Nashville: Abingdon Press, n.d.) 420. (Now published by Schmul Publishing Co.)

2. Adam Clarke, 409.

3. Albert Barnes, 47-48.

4. Matthew Poole, *Matthew-Revelation* vol. 3 in *Matthew Poole's Commentary on the Holy Bible* (Virginia Macdonald Pub. Co., n.d.) 214.

5. Ray Pritchard, *Names of the Holy Spirit* (Chicago: Moody Publishers, 1995) p. 35.

AUGUST

August 1

Music Was an Act of Creation (Part 1)

Genesis 1:1 — "In the beginning God created..."

Was music actually created as a part of God's objective acts of creation? Genesis 1:1 tells us, "In the beginning God created..." We know from the words *Elohiym bara eth* (430, 1254, 853) in verse one that the supreme, exceeding God made or created music from or of Himself. Some Christian music philosophers have believed that since music is "of or from God" that it was always a part of His moral nature and therefore did not have to be created in His objective acts of creation. They sometimes use John 1:3 — "All things were made by him; and without him was not any thing made that was made" — as support for their belief by saying that God only made things that needed to be made, but He did not need to make music, so He did not make it.

As I said earlier, this faulty belief is predicated on the theory that since music was already in, of, or from God, it was part of His moral nature at the time of the creation and therefore without the need of His creative work. I get blessed when I think about the fact that God wanted music enough to create it on purpose. I have no problem believing that He created music, giving Him ownership of it, returning my musical efforts to the God who created it.

Thought for the Day

Those who summarily dismiss what the Bible has to say about music normally believe that when the Bible mentions music, it is not really talking about the music part of music but rather about words, worship, diversity or anything but musical meaning. Therefore, they do not see any reason to place the music part of music under the lordship of Christ. So, to them, placing music and its beginning in the acts of a real creation is a superfluous exercise of over-zealous music philosophers.

Prayer for the Day

Lord, thank You for including music in Your creation. Thank You for making musicing unto God a means of grace to bring me closer unto You. Help me as I perform my vows unto You daily by praising Your name through music. This I pray in Your wonderful name. Amen.

August 2

Music Was an Act of Creation (Part 2)

Colossians 1:16 — "For by him were all things created, that are in heaven, and that are in earth, visible and invisible, whether they be thrones, or dominions, or principalities, or powers: all things were created by him, and for him."

God thought music into existence in His acts of creation. Because God created everything, music did not evolve into existence or come into existence as the results of man's efforts. Its origin is not the result of man's actions. Music was created in the original acts of creation. Any other belief is faulty and opens the door to music being or becoming an autonomous art form.

Most of the references to music in the Bible are found after the Genesis record. There is much that is still unknown about music in ancient Israel, but that is not an indication that what the Bible has recorded about music in ancient Israel is not important to Christian musicians today. So, you as a Christian musician can rejoice as you worship God today. Praise God, what He did in His acts of creation and what God's inspired Word teaches about music and musicing is valuable to you today.

Song for the Day

Guide Me O Thou Great Jehovah by W. Williams

Thought for the Day

If God thought about music "in the beginning" (and He most certainly did), and if God is "there" concerning music in this century (and He most certainly is), it is only logical to deduce that He still thinks about music. Smaller minds serve a smaller God who is perhaps too busy to think about music and musicing today or just doesn't care how we music unto Him. After all, haven't we grown up as Christian musicians until we can do this job all by ourselves? No, we have not. We need God, and we specifically need the guidance of the Holy Spirit when we music unto God. We also need the comfort and guiding power of what His written Word teaches us about music and musicing.

August 3

Music Was an Act of Creation (Part 3)

John 1:3 — "All things were made by him; and without him was not any thing made that was made."

As we discussed yesterday, some Christian music philosophers and practicing church musicians believe that music has evolved (from nothing to something) over the centuries and that it is the product of mankind rather than created by God on purpose. This faulty theory effectively lets the Christian musician who is seeking autonomy "off the hook" philosophically. If God did not objectively take nothing and make music out of this nothingness, then what does Psalm 146:6 mean when it so clearly states that it was God who "made heaven, and earth, the sea, and all that therein is: which keepeth truth forever"? Strong says that *asah* (6213) means "to do or make" something.

Is there any logical reason why music is not a part of this "all" which is mentioned here? Also, St. John 1:3 and 10, Ephesians 3:9 and Revelation 4:11 all support the belief of a complete creation and especially, Colossians 1:16— "For by him were all things created, that are in heaven, and that are in earth, visible and invisible, whether they be thrones, or dominions, or principalities, or powers: all things were created by him, and for him." As a committed Christian musician who has committed all sacred musicing to God for His honor and glory, you have a right to rejoice when you music unto Him.

Thought for the Day

I have always told my students that the term "evolved" is not the proper word to use when speaking about the development of music over the centuries. The word evolved has come to connote a musical "big bang" rather than the development of a God-created art form. An evolutionary process from "musical amoeba" to major symphony is a naive notion, rather than a fact grounded in our knowledge of ancient world music. The recent deciphering of the music of ancient Ugarit by the University of Berkley Department of Assyriology (Kilmer, *et al.*) and the deciphering of the *te'amim* below and above the OT Scripture (Suzanne Haik-Vantoura) has proven such notions to be entirely false. Because of the preciseness of both of these ancient notations, we know that at least some ancient music was highly developed. It strengthens my faith to know that ancient music was so developed and beautiful, and therefore, far from any "big bang."

Song for the Day

How Great Thou Art by Carl Boberg

August 4

Music Was an Act of Creation (Part 4)

Genesis 1:1-2 — "In the beginning God created the heaven and the earth. And the earth was without form, and void; and darkness was upon the face of the deep. And the Spirit of God moved upon the face of the waters."

I am drawn to the logical conclusion that out of the chaos, emptiness and confusion reported in verse two of Genesis chapter one, God created, and His creation included music. God chose to create music because, in His perfect will, He desired that it should be a part of His perfect creation.

In His objective acts of creation, God created the mathematical ratios that are the basis of what music is and what music will be like when a musician arranges the music part of music into artistic, musical patterns. Because of this, God has authority over how we organize and use His musical building blocks. When Christian musicians get rid of the sense of music ownership, many church music problems disappear.

If a Christian musician believes that God, in His infinite wisdom, created the building blocks of music, he or she should conclude that God has a will concerning the music building blocks that He created. Furthermore, it seems logical that if He had a will concerning the art form He created. He also has a perfect will concerning His creation. If He has a will concerning music, it is the responsibility of every Christian to study His Word to come to a more perfect understanding of how He wishes for us to worship Him with His wonderful creation. We should be reminded that it is the Christian musician's responsibility to "prove what is acceptable unto the Lord (Ephesians 5:10)." The "monkey" is on the ministering musician's back — not God's back!

Scripture for the Day

Romans 12:2 says, "And be not conformed to this world: but be ye transformed by the renewing of your mind, that ye may prove what is that good, and acceptable, and perfect, will of God."

Thought for the Day

God's Word is there to teach us, and the blessed Holy Spirit is there to guide and guard us, but we must do the proving.

August 5

Music Was an Act of Creation (Part 5)

Revelation 4:11 — "Thou art worthy, O Lord, to receive glory and honour and power: for thou hast created all things, and for thy pleasure they are and were created."

A nondescript and fuzzy music philosophy derived from a misunderstanding of the significance of Genesis 1:1 will give rise to a faulty musical ministry praxis. This means that if God, by virtue of ownership, does not become Lord over all of a Christian's musicing, as an art form and as a musical offering to God in that musician's music ministry, it will not be very long until God is not Lord at all over a Christian musician's musicing. It will not take very much time until a musician's music ministry will all become anthropocentric rather than Christocentric.

I recently read a book on worship that emphatically stated there should be no such thing as a Christian Music Philosophy. Perhaps the reason that church music is in such a mess in this century is that so many Christian musicians have decided not to decide. Such thinking is, without doubt, a philosophical belief, whether or not the musicians realize that it is. Of course, non-Christians do not believe that Christ should be at the center of a music philosophy. However, it is somewhat shocking to read the work of a Christian musician who has been squeezed into the world's mold philosophically.

Song for the Day

In Christ Alone by Stuart Townsend and Keith Getty

Thought for the Day

Christocentric music philosophy is not only expedient, it is a must if a Christian's music and musicing are going to be truly Christ-centered and if it has any hope of consistently following Bible principles of musicing unto God.

August 6

Music Was an Act of Creation (Part 6)

Colossians 1:16-18— "For by him were all things created, that are in heaven, and that are in earth, visible and invisible, whether they be thrones, or dominions, or principalities, or powers: all things were created by him, and for him: And he is before all things, and by him all things consist. And he is the head of the body, the church: who is the beginning, the firstborn from the dead; that in all things he might have the preeminence."

The English word preeminence means superiority, supremacy, greatness, distinction, prominence and predominance. Likewise the Greek word *proteuo* (4409) used in verse eighteen connotes that God must be first in authority. So, when the Word states that "in all things he might have the preeminence" it means just that—Christian musicians must submit because when it comes to music and musicing God has legitimate authority over the great art form He created. I have found that many times the more talented a musician is, the more trouble he or she has submitting.

Christian musicians must realize that they do not own music and recognize that they are musical servants with responsibilities rather than rights. Music was created because God willed that it should exist. Therefore, it is not far-fetched to come to the logical hypothesis that He still has a will concerning music. Again, we should remember that God created the formal properties of music (i.e., the nuts and bolts of music) that make it what it is capable of being. And someday, we will give a stewardship account of what we did with His musical building blocks.

Christian musicians must get rid of the sense of ownership of music and musicing. If a Christian owns music, he or she is truly an autonomous musician. If I own music, it is my music! I have rights concerning music because it is mine. If my music and the way I music is mine, then I have rights when it comes to my music. Since it is my music and my music ministry, I have the right to tell you that you are out of step with my musicing and if you do not like it you probably should worship somewhere else where you would be more comfortable. However, if I am a servant musician, I don't have any rights. I only have responsibilities when it comes to the music I utilize in worship.

Thought for the Day

I am here to be God's musical servant, so I must serve in the spirit of *sharath* (8334), i.e., like a menial worshipper, which means it is my responsibility to music in the spirit of humility.

August 7

Music Belongs to God

St. John 1:1, 3— "In the beginning was the Word... All things were made by him; and without him was not any thing made that was made."

It is comforting to a committed Christian musician when he or she realizes that music does not belong to any musician. God made music, so He owns it. The proper understanding of music begins with its ownership.

Music belongs to God because He created it in a real and personal way. He took nothing, and from Himself He created it—so, He owns it. Therefore, we need to realize that music did not begin with a "big bang" but rather with a big creation by a big creator. Knowing that God created and owns music helps the Christian musician to understand that, since He created music in a real and personal way, He still cares about music and how we use it.

As His musical servants, we are a part of something that God considered to be very good when He created it. Genesis 1:31 tells us very clearly, "And God saw everything that he had made, and, behold it was very good." Since music belongs to God, and since He created it in a very good condition, we know that He cares about what we do to His creation. Since He cares about what we do to music, we know that He will show us how to use it in accordance with the intent of its original "very good condition."

We are not alone in the twenty-first century. God has not abandoned us to wallow in ignorance concerning how to music. I Corinthians 2:16 tells us that we have the mind of Christ. It is, therefore, our responsibility to simply seek the spiritual discernment to gain the mind of Christ concerning how to music unto Him in this present age.

Song for the Day

How Great Thou Art by Carl Boberg

Thought for the Day

J.S. Bach wrote at the end of his compositions *soli Deo Gloria*, "solely to God alone." Is your musicing solely for the glory of God?

Prayer for the Day

Thank You, Lord, for creating music. Thank You for hovering over music in the twenty-first century. Thank You, blessed Holy Spirit, that You sometimes use music to draw men and women to Christ. Please help me to find the mind of Christ when I music unto You. Help me to music in such a way that You will be pleased with the condition of my musical offerings that I present to You. These things I pray in Your excellent name. Amen.

August 8

Believing What God has Said (Part 1)

Genesis 1:11, 13— "And God said, Let the earth bring forth grass, the herb yielding seed, and the fruit tree yielding fruit after his kind, whose seed is in itself, upon the earth: and it was so... And the evening and the morning were the third day."

The first chapter of the Book of Beginnings gives us a clear record of all the growing things created on the third day of creation. On the next day, God created the sun and the moon so that his creation would have the lights to sustain photosynthesis, which is essential to sustenance and growth of all the plant life He had created the day before.

Those who believe that each day of creation was at least a thousand or perhaps a million years apart have a hard time explaining scientifically how all those plants lived at least a thousand years without light. I guess they have faith that God suspended His laws of nature so that all those green things could exist until a thousand years or a million years had passed.

Christian musicians often get sucked into this non-literal view of the Genesis record, which leaves them ripe for all kinds of exotic hypotheses about theistic evolution. When one considers something in the Bible to be non-literal, then he or she needs to have a concrete reason why it is non-literal.

Why should we care? One of the reasons we should care is that if one starts to consider, without concrete logical reasoning, that the Bible record does not mean what it says—then there is no stopping place in such faulty logic. We should remember that the Word clearly asserts that the evening and the morning consisted of one day. Those who quote Psalm 90:4— " For a thousand years in thy sight are but as yesterday when it is past, and as a watch in the night" — as evidence against a six day creation are forgetting that we have no reason to assert when the Word states "the evening and the morning were the third day," that it is in any way referring to a thousand years.

Thought for the Day

There is a difference between interpreting the figurative language used in the Bible in a figurative manner and refusing to believe a direct statement given in the Bible in order to support a person's philosophy.

August 9

Believing What God has Said (Part 2)

Psalm 119:160— "Thy word is true from the beginning: and every one of thy righteous judgments endureth for ever."

Yesterday we started a discussion about believing the Genesis record. The Genesis record should be trusted to mean exactly what it states. That belief includes a real six-day creation. It takes blind faith to believe that the created plant life lived a thousand, or perhaps a million, years without sunlight.

Again, one may ask, "Why does a musician care whether creation took six days, six thousand or six million years?" A Christian musician cares because if one cannot trust the Genesis record, he or she will find it hard to trust the remaining Scriptures to be accurate. If the Bible is not accurate in what it says, then a Christian musician's truth basis fails.

It is no wonder that so many Christian musicians have trouble trusting what the Bible says about music and musicing unto God. Why should a musician trust what the Bible says about music if he or she cannot trust the Genesis record to be accurate? Remember that St. John 1:1 states, under the inspiration of the Holy Spirit that, "In the beginning was the Word, and the Word was with God, and the Word was God." This means that one cannot separate God from what He says. Before creation, Jesus was with God and was God. Therefore, we can trust every word about the creation of the world.

At this point you are probably wondering, "What is the devotional thought for the day?" The devotional thought is that "direction determines destiny." When a Christian musician goes down the philosophical path that "one cannot trust what is written in the Genesis record," then there is no stopping place and the result is believing that the Bible is not always accurate. With such a false philosophical basis, one erroneously concludes that the creation account is not literal, and therefore, not to be trusted.

If we are going to make it into the City of God, we are going to need the comfort, guidance, and hope of God's inspired Word. If we cannot trust His Word to be accurate, then we cannot trust what God has said to us. If one believes that part of it is accurate and other parts are not accurate, then just what part or parts can we trust?

Prayer for the Day

Lord, thank You for Your Word. Thank You that You are the Word! Thank You that no one can ever separate You from Your Word. I am asking You to help me to trust Your Word and help me to start trusting it in the

Genesis 1:1 account. Lord, I am asking You to help me not to be led astray by humanists, philosophers, agnostics, secular and theistic evolutionists. Please let the *logos Christos* dwell in my mind abundantly and in all wisdom, which the Holy Spirit teaches. These things I pray in Your reliable name. Amen.

August 10

Meditations that are Acceptable

Psalm 19:14— "Let the words of my mouth, and the meditation of my heart, be acceptable in thy sight, O Lord, my strength, and my redeemer."

The Hebrew word *higgaion* (1902), translated here in the AV as meditations, means a murmuring or solemn sound and is derived from *hagah* (1897), which means to meditate or ponder. I often hear musicians say that we are what we eat, but I do not often hear them say that we are what we muse or think. If a Christian musician muses on something long enough, he or she will believe it is true whether it is or not.

In this Psalm, David is asking YHVH to help him not to say or think anything that is not acceptable in God's sight. Words cut and kill, not only the person that we say them about, but also the person who says them. Thoughts cause actions that not only injure others, but also the person who thinks them.

In the thirteenth verse of this psalm, David also asks the LORD to forgive his hidden faults and his presumptuous (*zed* 2086) or proud sins. A musician must never let theology keep him or her from asking God for forgiveness for anything that would prevent that person from being upright, innocent or without moral blame before God.

Scripture for the Day

Philippians 4:8 says, "Finally, brethren, whatsoever things

are true, whatsoever things are honest, whatsoever things are just, whatsoever things are pure, whatsoever things are lovely, whatsoever things are of good report; if there be any virtue, and if there be any praise, think on these things."

Thought for the Day

Psalm 1:2 says, "But his delight is in the law of the LORD; and in his law doth he meditate day and night." If you meditate on the law of the Lord day and night, you will not have time to think on things that displease the Lord.

August 11

The Glory of the LORD

II Chronicles 5:13-14 — "…then the house was filled with a cloud, even the house of the LORD; So that the priests could not stand to minister by reason of the cloud: for the glory of the LORD had filled the house of God."

The Levites ministered on this occasion and, while they were musicing unto God, the glory of God filled the Temple. The priests could not carry out their duties and their sacrificial offerings. The sincere musicing of the Levite musicians and the priests' offerings gave way to a Divine visitation.

As the trumpeters and the singers thanked and praised YHVH for His goodness and His mercy, all of a sudden God's presence swept over the Temple. All those who were there knew that YHVH was tabernacling or inhabiting their musical and sacrificial worship.

Do you long for God's presence to fill the church when you have the responsibility and privilege to music unto Him? God will meet with us and will inhabit our praise if we seek Him with all our hearts. Psalm 22:3 says, "But thou art holy, O thou that inhabitest the praises of Israel." The most important part of our worship is turning our hearts toward God. Christian musicians have the responsibility to lead other Christians in taking the journey from the natural to the supernatural and experiencing communion with the blessed Trinity.

Song for the Day

We Have Come into Your House by B. Ballinger

Thought for the Day

If we want God's presence in our midst when we worship together, then we must make sure that we are getting along with each other.

Prayer for the Day

Lord, like the priests and the Levites in the ancient Jewish Temple, we want to thank You and praise You with our musical offerings. We are asking You to inhabit our praise and manifest Your presence in our musical worship. Lord, we confess that we do not know how to come in and go out before You. We want to please You with our worship, but we confess that we do not always know how to worship You. We want to thank You for the times that we feel Your presence as we music unto You. Help us to music in a way that will bring honor and glory to Your name. Amen.

August 12

Examine Yourselves

II Corinthians 13:5— "Examine yourselves, whether ye be in the faith; prove your own selves. Know ye not your own selves, how that Jesus Christ is in you, except ye be reprobates?"

Paul admonished the Corinthians to examine themselves to see if they were "in the faith." Although it is not healthy spiritually for Christian musicians to continually test themselves with "spiritual thermometers," it is a good thing to examine our spiritual lives periodically.

Paul, in Hebrews 3:6, admonishes Christians to "…hold fast the confidence and the rejoicing of the hope firm to the end." If Christ dwells in us, we should not ever surrender that faith. However, if a musician fails the spiritual test it is necessary to make the spiritual adjustments necessary to have peace with God. Paul was warning the Corinthians to do what was right when he stated in II Corinthians 13:7, "Now I pray to God that ye do no evil; not that we should appear approved, but that ye should do that which is honest…"

Regardless of one's theology, every Christian musician should admit that if he or she has sinned and come short of the glory of God, the blood of Jesus Christ only cleanses from all sin if we walk in the light (see I John 1:7). As I said before, continual, morbid spiritual introspection is not spiritually productive. However, a musician should never harbor, hide or try to rationalize away sin in his or her life.

Song for the Day

Satisfied with Jesus by B.B. McKinney

Thought for the Day

It is a good idea to spiritually examine ourselves occasionally, because it will help us to be sure that we are ready for the Great Judgment of God that will surely come after we leave this sinful world.

Prayer for the Day

Lord, I am asking You not to let me minister to others and become a spiritual castaway myself. Lord, please do not allow anything to come between my soul and You as my Savior. Will You take off the blinders, Lord, and let me see myself as You see me. These petitions I bring to You trusting that You are all-knowing. Amen.

August 13

If Any Lack Wisdom

James 1:5-6 — "If any of you lack wisdom, let him ask of God, that giveth to all men liberally, and upbraideth not; and it shall be given him. But let him ask in faith, nothing wavering. For he that wavereth is like a wave of the sea driven with the wind and tossed."

One has said that music ministry would be a perfect calling if we just didn't have to work with people. Of course, without people, we couldn't have corporate worship, congregational singing, choirs, church orchestras, vocal ensembles, or even a simple vocal or instrumental duet. People are the heart and soul of music ministry. Music ministry is not about the chief musician's plan, performance, position, or even his or her problems. Music ministry is about people lavishing praise upon the blessed Trinity.

Most of life's huge problems stem from working with people. Many of these problems require more wisdom than most of us have. So, what should we do? Ask God. He will supply the needed wisdom and won't chide, belittle, or make a joke of your asking for that wisdom.

There is one very important fact to remember when you ask God for wisdom. You must "…believe that he is, and that he is a rewarder of them that diligently seek him" (Hebrews 11:6).

Song for the Day

I Need Thee Every Hour by Annie S. Hawks

Thought for the Day

It is not a showing of inferiority or ineptness when a Chief Musician admits to God that he or she lacks wisdom to handle a certain situation.

Prayer for the Day

Lord, I am confessing that I do lack wisdom. I feel like Solomon of old who prayed, "...I know not how to go out or come in" (I Kings 3:7). Lord, help me to believe and trust that You really will give me the necessary wisdom to work with others and to be a good and faithful music minister. These things I pray in Your name. Amen.

August 14

How Should We Then Sing?

I Corinthians 14:15— "What is it then? I will pray with the spirit, and I will pray with the understanding also: I will sing with the spirit, and I will sing with the understanding also."

How should we then pray and sing unto God? It seems that Christian musicians tend to identify more with singing and praying with the Spirit than praying and singing with the intellect. It doesn't have to be either-or but rather a wise balance of both. If praying and musicing are to have the proper balance, they must utilize both Spirit (*pneuma* 4551) and intellect (*nous* 3563).

If our musicing is going to be effectual, we need the anointing of the Holy Spirit. However, it is difficult for the Holy Spirit to bless and anoint our musicing unless we engage our mind. Our musical offering must include passion, thought, feeling, vitality, believability and mental understanding if it is to have real meaning.

Remember that "The husbandman that laboureth must be first partaker of the fruits" (II Timothy 2:6). Christian musicians must be fed spiritually before they can feed others with their musical offerings. It is only when the Christian musician's soul is fed that he or she will have a real spiritual understanding of the message of the music being presented to God. So, efficacious musicing requires the aid and anointing of the Holy Spirit on the musician's intellectual musical offering.

Song for the Day

Spirit of God, Descend upon My Heart by G. Croly

Prayer for the Day

Lord, please give me the power of the Holy Spirit so that my musicing will truly be with Spirit and with understanding. This I pray in Your name. Amen.

August 15

Submit and Resist

James 4:7-8 — "Submit yourselves therefore to God. Resist the devil, and he will flee from you. Draw nigh to God, and he will draw nigh to you..."

If the Christian musician is going to be an overcomer he or she must resist and submit at the same time. However, you cannot resist until you submit. When you submit it is easier to resist. God will give you the power to resist Satan, but He will only give you that power if you submit to Him.

Submitting every situation to God is, at times, a difficult task. Many Christian musicians are energetic self-starters who are not often of a mind to let someone else solve their problems. They know that God is able to solve life situations, but they still try to deal with their problems without fully submitting to God's will and wisdom.

How should we then submit? The answer is found in verse eight. Draw near to God! The closer that a Christian musician gets to the great heart of God, the easier it becomes to submit to His will and way. The closer a Christian draws to God, the closer He comes to the submitted musician. The closer a Christian comes to God, the more he or she is able to take advantage of God's wisdom and protection. Satan does not like to be in the presence of God, so as we draw near to God, Satan will flee from us.

Song for the Day

I Surrender All by Judson Van Denter

Thought for the Day

If you have trouble submitting to the Lord, try getting out of the driver's seat.

Prayer for the Day

Lord, I am asking You to help me to submit to Your will and accept Your protection from Satan. Help me to draw near to You so that I can hear Your voice and be able to resist Satan's temptations, accusations, deceptions and powers. Help me to recognize that You have promised to draw near to me if I will draw near to You. Help me to claim Your promise that when I resist Satan in Your wonderful and powerful name that he will have to flee from me. Thank You, Lord, for Your constant protection. These things I pray in Your name. Amen.

August 16

Doing God's Will from the Heart

Ephesians 6:6-7 — "Not with eyeservice, as menpleasers; but as the servants of Christ, doing the will of God from the heart; With good will doing service, as to the Lord, and not to men."

Today is my daughter Sarah's birthday. Sarah means lady, princess, or noblewoman in Hebrew. As you will remember, God changed the name of Sarai, the wife of Abraham in the Old Testament, to Sarah. She became the mother of

Isaac at the age of 90. Isaac was the first one to be born in the Abrahamic covenant.

Sarah has always been our princess. She has always been a lady of which I could be proud. The dictionary defines a princess as a woman regarded as having the status or qualities of royalty. To me, that explains the qualities of our daughter Sarah. She has always been a noble lady because, from the time that she was a small girl, she desired to please her parents, and more important, she desired to please God. In my opinion, the noblest thing that a Christian can do is find and do the will of God.

So, the point of this little devotional today is that, in my opinion, if you want to be a noble man or noble woman, give your heart to Jesus and seek to find and do His will. Our world is consumed by the importance of being engaged in the so-called noble professions. To many post-postmoderns, the noblest professions are those which will provide the most material wealth. However, they are mistaken, because the most important and noble thing that any Christian can do is to find and do God's will. We should all remember that, as 1 John 2:17 reminds us, "… the world passeth away, and the lust thereof: but he that doeth the will of God abideth for ever."

August 17

God Hears Us

Psalm 5:2-3— "Hearken unto the voice of my cry, my King [*Melek* 4428], and my God [*Elohiym* 430]: for unto thee will I pray. My voice shalt thou hear in the morning O Lord; in the morning will I direct my prayer unto thee, and will look up."

This Psalm of David, addressed to the Chief Musician, was written to YHVH. The Psalm opens by David petitioning God to hear his prayer and, furthermore, for

YHVH to consider the psalmist's meditation or musing. He recognizes who God is as he calls Him *Melek Elohiym*, i.e., King and Supreme God.

When a musician earnestly petitions God, he or she must believe that He is the supreme and only God and King. However, if the answer does not come quickly, this musician must approach prayer as David did on this occasion. David looked up to God and determined that the LORD would hear his voice every morning and that his petition would be directed to the one who could answer his prayer. So, look up, musician! The fact that your prayer has not been answered yet does not mean that it will not be answered. God answers prayer, and He will answer your prayers if you pray and look up to Him in faith.

Song for the Day

Sweet Hour of Prayer by W. Walford

Prayer for the Day

LORD, I may not hear from You every day, but I want You to hear from me every day. I want to thank You in advance for hearing my sincere petition. I am looking "up" to You because You are willing and able to answer my prayer. LORD, I pray that Your will be done in this matter. Help me to desire Your will instead of mine. Thank You, LORD, for past prayers You have heard and answered. Thank You that You are concerned about my problems and perplexities. These things I pray in Your wonderful name. Amen.

August 18

Ministry that is Sounding Brass

I Corinthians 13:1— "Though I speak with the tongues of men and of angels, and have not charity, I am become as sounding brass, or a tinkling cymbal."

The sounding brass (*echo chalkos* — 2278, 5475) was no doubt referring to a series of hollow brass vases found in niches in Greek theaters. They were tuned chromatically to amplify the actor's and singer's voices. However, these vases gave off an unnatural sound. Likewise, the tinkling or clanging cymbals (*alalazo kumbalon* — 214, 2950) produced a clanging hollow sound. So, our musical ministry, unless it is bathed in prayer, humility and agape love is of little effectiveness.

The musician who makes the loudest noise is not necessarily the most spiritual or effective music minister. Enthusiasm is no substitute for the *dunamis* (1411) of the Spirit. Likewise, the most astute performer or director does not always have the most efficacious music ministry. Church musicians and worshippers, in general, want to be effectively led in worship. However, one must not only lead with skill but also with spiritual passion. Without the power (*dunamis*) of the Holy Spirit, religious musicing becomes a hollow, empty musical offering.

Song for the Day

Love Divine All Loves Excelling by Charles Wesley

Thought for the Day

If we really love God, we will act. Real love is love in action. If I see that you are hurting one of my grandchildren, I will act because I really love them.

August 19

Musicians are Sometimes Depressed

I Samuel 16:17-18 — "And Saul said unto his servants, Provide me now a man that can play well, and bring him to me. Then answered one of the servants, and said, Behold, I have seen a son of Jesse the Bethlehemite, that is cunning in playing, and a mighty valiant man, and a man of war, and prudent in matters, and a comely person, and the LORD is with him."

When God allowed the evil spirit to trouble Saul, the king sought out a musician who could play skillfully and beautifully (*nagan yatab*—5059, 3190). We know from this account that there was more involved in David's playing than mere performance, because the eighteenth verse tells us that "the LORD was with him." However, David was given the opportunity to minister musically to the king because he was a cunning player of the harp.

Christian musicians who have had a long, broad, dedicated study of applied music are often prone to depression. They often wonder, "Why do I work so hard on perfecting my instrument if I'm not a professional concert musician?" Every Christian musician should remember that one does not have to be a great musician to be a useful or successful musician in God's eyes.

Do not let Satan make you think that you are not "good enough" to be used of God. Do not let the enemy of your soul depress and accuse you. It is a fact that the longer you study music, the more you will realize just how much you do not know about it. However, you do not serve Jesus Christ with what you do not know but rather with what you do know. Also, remember that the Lord did not say, "Well done thou talented and accomplished servant," but rather, "Well done thou good and faithful servant." However, that is not to say that it is not necessary for the Christian musician to be prepared musically. As Christian musicians we should remember that David was not only an accomplished musician, i.e., "cunning in playing," but also the inspired writer recorded that "the LORD is with him."

Thought for the Day

King Saul sought out a godly musician that could play beautiful music and play it skillfully to help him get out of his depressed state. Often God opens doors for music ministry in accordance with the musician's musical and spiritual preparation.

August 20

To the Chief Musician

I Chronicles 15:22 — "And Chenaniah, chief of the Levites, was for song: he instructed about the song, because he was skilful."

Chenaniah was in charge of music, and he had a burden (*massa* 4853) for music in worship. He was placed in charge because of his burden for song and because he was a skillful (*biyn* 995) musician. If you are reading this devotional today and you are a skillful musician, it is your responsibility to use your musical skills for God. You may be so emotionally and physically weary that you sometimes wish that you could run away and hide in a very large church where no one knows that you are an experienced, accomplished musician.

As we mentioned above, Chenaniah was not only "in charge" of music, but he also ministered with great *massa,* or burden, borne in upon him of God. The Hebrew word *massa* used here is the same one used of the major prophets of the Bible who were said to have this burden borne in upon them by God. You, as a Christian musician, have not only the responsibility of ministering through the art of music, but you also have the responsibility to carry a spiritual burden for the musicians you minister with and the people you minister to.

Song for the Day

I Will Serve Thee by Howard Walter

Thought for the Day

It seems that God gives a "burden for song" to those whom

He can trust to serve Him with their musicing.

Prayer for the Day

Lord, I confess that sometimes I feel like quitting, but I know that I can't because You have called me to minister musically for You. Holy Spirit, I am asking that You will fill me afresh with Your anointing and power for service. Help me to music with a burden for lost souls, weary Christians, babes in Christ, skeptics and seekers who come under the sound of my music ministry and young, talented musicians. Help me never to give up or lose hope on the inside. These petitions I bring to You who are exceedingly able to give more than I could ever ask or think. I love You, Lord, and I want to be Your musical servant as long as You give me breath. Amen.

August 21

The Word Was and Is God

St. John 1:1-2— "In the beginning was the Word, and the Word was with God, and the Word was God. The same was in the beginning with God."

St. John refers to Jesus Christ as the Word. He also tells us, under the inspiration of the Holy Spirit, that Jesus Christ was before creation, because verse two tells us that He, the Word, "was in the beginning with God" and that "All things were made by Him." Thus, John establishes that Jesus is God the third person of the Trinity and that He cannot be separated from the *logos* or Word.

Those of us who have been born again are adopted sons and daughters of God, because "...as many as received him, to them gave he power to become the sons of God, even to them that believe on his name" (John 1:12). Every Christian musician should receive strength in the knowledge that the Word assures us that the Holy Spirit

"...beareth witness with our spirit, that we are the children of God" (Romans 8:16).

At times in the past, when I could not feel God's presence when I was praying, I have experienced Him through reading the Bible. If you are having trouble experiencing God's presence, try reading His Word and singing Scripture songs.

Song for the Day

Jesus the Very Thought of Thee by Bernard of Clairvaux

Thought for the Day

Since I am truly God's child, I can talk to Him like I would talk to my earthly father.

Prayer for the Day

Heavenly Father, I want to love You and experience You more in my times of private devotions. Please reveal Yourself to me through prayer and reading Your Word. Lord, I am Yours and You are mine since You have adopted me as Your son. Thank You for making me Your child. I gratefully pray in Your wonderful name. Amen.

August 22

God Really Does Care

Hebrews 4:15 — "For we have not an high priest which cannot be touched with the feeling of our infirmities; but was in all points tempted like as we are, yet without sin."

The Greek word *asthenia* (769) translated infirmities in the AV means feebleness, moral frailty or weakness. Have you ever felt like you had so displeased God because of your spiritual failure that you could not touch Him? Have you ever come to Him at the end of a frustrating busy week so ashamed that you had almost left Christ out of your difficult week? I have! I have come to Him after I had failed the test, begging Him for forgiveness. I know in retrospect that I have not always understood just how much Jesus had been touched with the feeling of my infirmity and spiritual weakness. I was unaware that even though I had failed to ask Him for help, He had been helping me through the time of frustration and trouble.

Musicians are most often very busy people. They are many times engulfed in "doing" rather than "being." They are often so busy trying to be a ministering musician that they fail to lean on our very wise and loving heavenly Father. Christian musicians need to be reminded often that our high priest, Jesus Christ, is very approachable. However, we must remember to draw near Him if we want His help.

Song for the Day

A Mighty Fortress is Our God by Martin Luther

Thought for the Day

We all need to remember that the just live by faith in God alone, and not by works, i.e., not by doing. That being said, James 2:26 reminds Christians, "For as the body without the spirit is dead, so faith without works is dead also."

Prayer for the Day

Great and wise High Priest, You understand my temptations and infirmities because You went through them without ever sinning. I am asking You, right now, to please help me to recognize and acknowledge Your presence. Help me to make a practice of constantly recognizing Your presence in my life. Please help me to be willing to listen to Your voice. I know that You not only listen, but You also love, restore, heal and forgive those who truly ask of You. Please lift me up in the most holy faith and help me to put on the whole armor of God so that I may be able to resist Satan. I pray in Your name. Amen.

August 23

Sometimes Musicians are Happy

James 5:13 — "Is any among you afflicted? let him pray. Is any merry? let him sing psalms."

James must have understood musicians when he alluded to the fact that when they are afflicted, undergo hardship, suffer misunderstanding, trouble, or are in trouble of their own making, they need to pray. He believed in the benefits of prayer because he later stated in James 5:16 that efficacious prayer is powerful! Christian musicians do not seem to hesitate to ask God for "stuff" because it seems that they are almost always in need. It is one thing for a musician to ask, but it is entirely another to believe that "the effectual fervent prayer of a righteous man availeth much" (James 5:16).

Many times musicians look like they are sad when they are in need. However, Christian musicians are not always sad. Sometimes, believe it or not, they are happy. When they are happy, what should they do? James, writing under Divine inspiration, declared that they should sing psalms. Some authors render the Greek word *psallo* (5567) translated psalms in this verse in the AV, as "to sing a hymn" or to "celebrate the praises of God in song." The word *psallo* actually means to "twitch or twang," i.e., touch the parts of a stringed instrument. So, it may be justly rendered that happy Christian musicians should sing songs accompanied by stringed instruments.

The point that James was making was that musicians naturally sing the praises of God when they are happy. Unfortunately, Christian musicians, happy or not, often sing out of a sense of duty rather than from a grateful, happy heart. Musicing is a "job" to them. What a pity that they often miss the joy of simply musicing for joy unto the Lord.

Song for the Day

I Love You Lord by L. Klein

Thought for the Day

I used to sing to my college choir, "If you're happy and you know it, show your face. If you're happy and you know it, show your face. If you're happy and you know it, then your face will surely show it. So, if you're happy and you know it, show your face."

Prayer for the Day

Lord, I want to take time right now to thank You for the gift of music! Thank You for the inner and outward joy You give to Your happy musicians who are Your children. Please help me to never merely music unto You with a sense of duty as I carry out my calling and profession. Help me to daily experience the joy of simply musicing unto You out of a happy passionate heart filled with love and gratitude. This I am praying in Your matchless name. Amen.

August 24

God has Not Forgotten You

Genesis 4:21— "And his brother's name was Jubal: he was the father of all such as handle the harp and organ."

Genesis 4:21 has the distinction of being the first reference to music in the Holy Writ. Among those names most anciently mentioned in Scripture, Jubal is listed. Not only is this musician listed, but he is also called *ab* (01) which is the primitive Hebrew and Chaldean word for father, chief, and principal person.

Musicians soar to the seventh heaven during their musicing unto God and plunge to the abyss of despair after church is over. While reflecting on the worship service, they only remember that the two main bass singers and the soprano soloist didn't show up for morning service. Furthermore, the tenors sang flat and hardly anyone said thank you after church was over!

One way of looking at it is that poor Jubal only got one tiny verse in all of the Old Testament. However, you could look at it that his name and what he did was inscribed in the inspired Genesis Record. Man would forget him, but God will not let us forget His musician. Not only do we remember Jubal as a musician, but as the "father" of musicians.

If you are a musician and you are reading this devotional, I do not need to draw you a picture. You know what I mean. God has not forgotten you. God loves you and He remembers all your service to Him.

Song for the Day

Close to Thee by F.J. Crosby

Thought for the Day

I once heard R.G. Flexon say, "If God can keep me all these years, He can keep you from one revival to the next."

Prayer for the Day

Forgive me, Lord, for feeling alone and forgotten. Cleanse me from self-pity and the sin of mistrusting that You will remember me. You have promised to be a friend that "sticketh closer than a brother" (Proverbs 18:24).

August 25

Songs of Deliverance

Psalm 32:7 — "Thou art my hiding place; thou shalt preserve me from trouble; thou shalt compass me about with songs of deliverance. Selah."

The psalmist David recognized that YHVH the self-existent, eternal God who is, was his source of protection. He referred to the LORD as his "hiding place." The Hebrew word *cether* (5643), which is translated hiding place in the AV, means a covering. Furthermore, the psalmist recognized God as his "preserver" (*natsar* 5341), i.e., one who guards, protects or keeps.

How does God keep us from trouble or in the time of trouble? David declares under the inspiration of the Holy Spirit that "thou shalt compass [surround] me about with songs of deliverance." Psalm 3:2-3 reminds us all that times of trouble will come and that "Many there be which say of my soul, There is no help for him in God. Selah. But thou, O LORD, art a shield for me; my glory, and the lifter up of mine head."

I do not know how many times I have said that Christian musicians often believe that "we are what we eat," but they less often understand that we are "what we think." Christian musician, what kind of songs have you placed in your mind? In the time of trouble, God's Word declares that the Lord will surround you with "songs of deliverance." That is— He will if you know any songs of deliverance.

Song for the Day

I Have Found a Hiding Place by C.F. Weigle

Thought for the Day

With every temptation God has provided a way of escape (I Corinthians 10:13). However, it is your responsibility to escape.

Prayer for the Day

Lord, please help me to fill my mind with songs that bring honor to You. Help me to fill my mind with the *logos Christos* so that You may use these to deliver me in the time of trouble. Amen.

August 26

Worship God in This Place

Genesis 28:16— "And Jacob awaked out of his sleep, and he said, Surely the LORD is in this place; and I knew it not."

Jacob's early adult life was plagued with mistakes and failures. He was so busy being a supplanter or schemer that he could not hear the voice of God. After Jacob had lied to his father and had to leave home to protect his life, he finally came to his senses. In a dream, Jacob was able to hear the voice of God. The Lord said to him, "I am YHVH Elohim." I am the self-existent, eternal God who is, and I am the supreme exceeding God!

Christian musician, don't become so busy "doing" that you don't have time to "be." Don't merely lead others in worship. Make sure that you worship God every day. Learn to recognize even the little things that God does for you day by day. Make sure you turn your pillow into an altar. Anoint it with the oil of your tears as you worship the supreme, self-existent, eternal God who is. Learn to recognize as you experience worship that "surely the LORD is in this place."

Song of the Day

Holy Ground by Geron Davis

Thought for the Day

It is difficult to meet God at your private altar if you don't have one.

Prayer for the Day

Lord, forgive me for becoming so busy leading others in worship that I don't worship. Help me to turn my pillow into an altar and help me to recognize Your presence which is all around me today.

August 27

God Hears Our Music

Exodus 32:18 — "And he said, It is not the voice of them that shout for mastery, neither is it the voice of them that cry for being overcome: but the noise of them that sing do I hear."

As Moses came down from the mountain with the Decalogue, Joshua said to Moses, "There is the noise of war in the camp." Moses recognized the music to be depressing, bleating, noisy singing (*kowl 6983, anah 6031*). Some Bible historians believe that these people were worshipping and dancing (vs. 19) naked (vs. 25) around the golden calf with raucous music.

They were worshipping an idol. No wonder this worship was accompanied by "noisy singing" and "naked dancing." Not everything that went on in ancient worship music was of God. Likewise, not everything that goes on in postmodern and post-postmodern musical worship is of God. Beware, chief musician, that you do not get squeezed into the world's mold of musicing. These Israelites, whose hearts were full of carnality, were dancing and yelling to the noise of their music. This type of worship, which made no distinction between the sacred and the profane, seemed to them to be the proper thing to do.

Today if a Christian musician believes that there is a difference between the sacred and the profane, he or she may be laughed to scorn. Nevertheless, it made a difference then and it still makes a difference today. Chief musician, "guard your musicing." "Walk circumspectly" and "prove what is acceptable unto the Lord." When you face Him whose eyes are as a flame of fire, you will be glad you did.

Song for the Day

I Will Sing of My Redeemer by P.P. Bliss

Thought for the Day

I remember hearing Reverend John Page, Sr. saying, "You need to develop a backbone like a saw log if you plan to make it into the City of God."

Prayer for the Day

Lord, "I count not myself to have apprehended." Please give me the wisdom to discern between music that is sacred and profane. Do not let me get squeezed into the world's mode of musicing. I am asking in Your wise name. Amen.

August 28

Compose, Teach, and Sing the Songs of Jehovah

Deuteronomy 31:19 — "Now therefore write ye this song for you, and teach it the children of Israel: put it in their mouths, that this song may be a witness for me against the children of Israel."

The children of Israel had, time after time, forgotten the goodness of YHVH and had turned to the false gods of their neighbors. In verse 16, God told Moses that it would not be long until Israel would again go after false gods.

God has always been faithful to His people, so once again

He sent his man with a message. It was a song (see Deuteronomy 32). The purpose of this song was to witness against an apostatizing nation.

The musician was first to compose a song, second to teach it to them and third to have them sing it. It is never sufficient to "talk" the songs of the LORD. They must be sung. Now, song leader, you know a little more why we sing the *logos Christos* in church. God has given musicians the solemn opportunity and responsibility to compose, teach, and sing the songs of the LORD.

Not all songs that should be sung in church will be "hippity-hop over the top." Some of them will be, "Are You Living Where God Answers Prayer?" "A Charge to Keep I Have," "Nothing Between My Soul and the Savior," and "Guard Your Heart." Whether our music is a simple praise chorus or a serious song about God's judgment of the wicked, we should count it a privilege to catechize those who attend our church services with the songs of our precious Lord and Savior Jesus Christ.

Song for the Day

Teach Me Thy Way, O Lord by B.M. Ramsey

Thought for the Day

If your musicing is going to be didactic, it must have enough content and depth to teach something worthwhile. Avoid spaghetti music—music that is very long and not very deep.

Prayer for the Day

Lord, help me to be holy and to help others to love You in a greater way. May my musicing unto God be a means of grace to me and to those to whom I minister. I ask in the fear of the almighty God. Amen.

August 29

Who can Find Such a Woman?

Proverbs 31:10-14 — "Who can find a virtuous woman? for her price is far above rubies. The heart of her husband doth safely trust in her, so that he shall have no need of spoil. She will do him good and not evil all the days of her life. She seeketh wool, and flax, and worketh willingly with her hands. She is like the merchants' ships; she bringeth her food from afar."

Today is my wife Sheila's birthday. When I thought about writing something for this day, the above passage from Proverbs immediately came to my mind. She is all of the above and much more. She is the reason that we could live well on a very careful budget during the years that our four children were growing up. She has been a wonderful wife and an excellent, wise mother to our children.

How can all this be possible? When I think about her, I am reminded of Proverbs 31:25, "Strength and honour are her clothing; and she shall rejoice in time to come." Certainly, my wife, Sheila can rejoice in our children. Only God knows how great her reward will be in heaven for the wisdom and love that she exhibited in our home.

Furthermore, as Proverbs 31:27 explains, "She looketh well to the ways of her household, and eateth not the bread of idleness." Never has there ever been a wife and mother who was a harder worker than her. So, today I ask the same question as the wisest man that ever lived asked in Proverbs 31:10 — "Who can find a virtuous woman? For her price is far above rubies."

Prayer for the Day

Lord, I am asking You to especially bless all the mothers who are ministering musicians. Thank You for mothers who are willing to practice music with their children. Thank You for mothers who are willing to make their children practice. Thank You for mothers who teach their children at an early age to minister musically during their early childhood. Lord, please give these mothers strength to provide musically for their children. Lord, lift these mothers in the most holy faith so that they may be a life-long example of an unselfish Christian musician. This I am praying in Your holy Name. Amen

August 30

Such as Taught to Sing Praise

2 Chronicles 23:13— "And she looked, and, behold, the king stood at his pillar at the entering in, and the princes and the trumpets by the king: and all the people of the land rejoiced, and sounded with trumpets, also the singers with instruments of musick, and such as taught to sing praise..."

Among those who were worshipping was a classification of Levite musicians whose occupational specialty was teaching others to sing praise to YHVH. Maybe the reason that there are so many musicians who present God with musical offerings that are less than excellent, and certainly not appropriate for public worship, is that no one in their church fellowship has ever bothered to teach them how to sing praises unto our awesome and holy heavenly Father.

Those of you who are teaching little children to sing Scripture songs and praise choruses are doing the future church and God's kingdom a great service. Others may not understand the importance of what you are doing. However, God thought it was important to teach others to "sing praise," because He made specific mention of it in His inspired Word.

Thought for the Day

Christian fellowships need many more Christian musicians who will take the time and effort to teach young Christians how to music unto God.

Song for the Day

Praise Him, All Ye Little Children, anonymous

Prayer for the Day

Precious Lord, I am asking You to pour out a special blessing on all of Your musical servants who teach little children to praise You with their musicing. Wherever these special music servants are today, please surround them with Your love and grace and help them to reach out to You and receive anointing and power for this special musical service to You. Lift them before You and make them aware of Your understanding and love for the musical ministry they perform. Help them to raise generations of Christians who will "know the joyful sound" and will know how to music unto You in this century. I am asking in Your great and awesome name. Amen.

August 31

The Christian Musician has an Advocate

Arise My Soul Arise

Arise, my soul, arise; shake off thy guilty fears;
The bleeding Sacrifice in my behalf appears:
Before the throne, my surety stands,
Before the throne, my surety stands,
My name is written on His hands.

He ever lives above, for me to intercede;
His all-redeeming love, His precious blood to plead:
His blood atoned for all our race,

His blood atoned for all our race,
And sprinkles now the throne of grace.

Five bleeding wounds He bears, received on Calvary;
They pour effectual prayers; they strongly plead for
   me:
"Forgive him, oh, forgive," they cry,
"Forgive him, oh, forgive," they cry,
"Nor let that ransomed sinner die!"

The Father hears Him pray, His dear anointed One;
He cannot turn away the presence of His Son;
His Spirit answers to the blood,
His Spirit answers to the blood,
And tells me I am born of God.

My God is reconciled; His pard'ning voice I hear;
He owns me for His child; I can no longer fear:
With confidence I now draw nigh,
With confidence I now draw nigh,
And "Father, Abba, Father," cry.
                              —CHARLES WESLEY (1742)

I John 4:18 states, "There is no fear in love; but perfect love casteth out fear: because fear hath torment. He that feareth is not made perfect in love." Yet Wesley wrote, "Shake off thy guilty fears." He recognized that the enemy of the Christian musician's soul would often tempt him or her with "fears". Wesley knew that Christ who bled and died as the sacrifice for our sins, as Romans 8:34 attests, "…is even at the right hand of God, who also maketh intercession for us."

Hebrews 12:2 also states that we must look "…unto Jesus the author and finisher of our faith; who for the joy that was set before him endured the cross, despising the shame, and is set down at the right hand of the throne of God. " Part of what our divine paraclete does for Christian musicians to intercede for us, like Jesus promised Peter in Luke 22:31 states, "…Satan hath desired to have you, that he may sift you as wheat: But I have prayed for thee, that thy faith fail not…"

It is true that the Christian musician cannot make it to heaven without our Savior's continuous help. However, Wesley reminds us in verse 3 that "The Father hears Him pray, His dear anointed One; He cannot turn away the presence of His Son." Most of us have times when we recognize very clearly that we are weak and are in need of God's grace. Christ is our surety when he prays for us, "'Forgive him, oh, forgive,' they [his wounds] cry, 'Forgive him, oh, forgive,' they cry, 'Nor let that ransomed sinner die!'"

Wesley understood Romans 8:16— "The Spirit itself beareth witness with our spirit, that we are the children of God…"— when he wrote, "My God is reconciled; His pard'ning voice I hear; He owns me for His child; I can no longer fear: With confidence I now draw nigh, With confidence I now draw nigh, And 'Father, Abba, Father,' cry."

So, Christian musician, your assurance of salvation does not rest in yourself but rather in the efficacious blood of Jesus Christ. Right now, shake off any fears that you have, as Hebrews 12:2 admonishes, "Looking unto Jesus the author and finisher of our faith; who for the joy that was set before him endured the cross, despising the shame, and is set down at the right hand of the throne of God."

Song for the Day

I Need Thee Every Hour by Annie Hawkes

Thought for the Day

Hebrews 4:15 states, "For we have not an high priest which cannot be touched with the feeling of our infirmities; but was in all points tempted like as we are, yet without sin." Thank God today that you have a sinless Savior to be your advocate today.

SEPTEMBER

September 1

Ancient Bible Landmarks of Musicing

Proverbs 22:28 — "Remove not the ancient landmark, which thy fathers have set."

This verse in the Book of Proverbs is a reference to the subject matter of the nineteenth chapter of Deuteronomy. No doubt the reason that this admonition was given in Proverbs 22:28 is that if they were to remove the ancient landmarks, the people's inheritance would be in danger of being destroyed. The danger was not only to the present generation but for all generations that would follow.

Everyone who works in churches, Christian colleges or Christian schools must deal with preserving the ancient landmarks of Christian faith and practice. Christian musicians are responsible for the practice of music. Not only does church music matter, but the practice of how we music unto God matters. Imagine the God who spoke worlds into existence and created music in a real way, not caring about the practice of musicing unto Him. It should not be a novel thought to Christian musicians that music matters to God. He not only cares about music but also how we music unto Him. Therefore, all church musicians will give an account of how they, and the musicians under their hands, music unto God.

So what is the point? The point is that there are ancient landmarks given in the Bible of how we should music unto God. Therefore it behooves all Christian musicians to study God's Word so that we may preserve these ancient landmarks of musicing unto the Triune God.

Song for the Day

A Charge to Keep I Have by Charles Wesley

Thought for the Day

Can you imagine that the God who spoke music into existence doesn't care what we do with it?

Prayer for the Day

Lord, help me to understand the over six-hundred references to music in Your Word, so that I may serve You with music. Please help me to preserve the ancient landmarks of musicing, so that those who come behind me will find me to have been faithful in my examples of musicing unto You. Amen.

September 2

A Heart Made Ready

Romans 8:38-39— "For I am persuaded, that neither death, nor life, nor angels, nor principalities, nor powers, nor things present, nor things to come, nor height, nor depth, nor any other creature, shall be able to separate us from the love of God, which is in Christ Jesus our Lord."

It is no mystery that in death, we can be separated from God if we are not prepared spiritually to meet Him. However, life many times separates Christian musicians from God. Living does not have to pull us away from God, but it can! The cares of this life can slowly, but surely, move us further and further away from God. On the contrary, living each moment in the hollow of His mighty hand can draw us closer to our heavenly Father.

This scripture passage also warns us that created things can separate us from God if we let them. Music is a created thing, for we know that in the beginning, God created music. Music, a created thing, has drawn many Christians' hearts away from God.

When Christian musicians worship music instead of using it as a means of grace to draw closer to Christ, music becomes a god — an idol. Christian musicians must remember the commandment, "Thou shalt have no other gods before me" (Exodus 20:3).

God will not share His glory with a practicing musician hawking his or her artistic wares in front of the body of Christ. If we as musicians want to be "more than conquerors," we will use musicing as a means of grace and never as a means to draw attention to ourselves or the art of music.

Song for the Day

Close to Thee by Fanny Crosby

Thought for the Day

Christians do not worship music. They worship God with music. It is one of the ways a Christian responds to God.

Prayer for the Day

Lord, I know that I will come through all things by the power of the indwelling Spirit, not my talent or my musical performance. Father, teach me how to draw closer to You and to lead others into a closer walk with You by musicing unto God. Amen.

September 3

Fixing the Musician's Heart

II Chronicles 25:2 — "And he did that which was right in the sight of the LORD, but not with a perfect heart.

King Amaziah started out following what was written in the book of Moses. He was, in the beginning, a good king. He tried to do right and the biblical record says he did do right. But not with a perfect heart. The Hebrew word *Shalem* (8003) connotes a complete, perfect, peaceable heart that was made ready to properly serve Jehovah.

One of Satan's traps for Christian musicians is to get them so busy "doing" that they lose sight of "being." It is one thing to "do" the service of God, but entirely another to "be" a true follower of Christ.

Amaziah's heart was not fixed upon YHVH. He started his reign following the Lord (vs. 27) but "he brought the gods of the children of Seir, and set them up to be his gods" (vs. 14).

Christian musicians who do not settle all the issues of the heart often get sidetracked and sooner or later fail. We must be sure that we deal with all of the issues of the heart and "lay aside every weight, and the sin which doth so easily beset us..."

Song for the Day

I Want to Be Like Jesus by T.O. Chisholm

Thought for the Day

"God wants deep heart change not just behavior modification." (Reverend T. Keep)

Prayer for the Day

Lord, please do not let me become so busy "doing" that I forget about "being" a Christian. Please let me see the worst of the issues of my heart now— not later— or when it is too late. Help me to not only do that which is right, but help me to do so with a perfect heart. Amen.

September 4

Song Leaders are Ministering Servants

Psalm 47:6-7— "Sing praises to God, sing praises: sing praises unto our King, sing praises. For God is the King of all the earth: sing ye praises with understanding."

This psalm is addressed to the chief musician. All the people are admonished to recognize who God is and what He does for us. However, it is the chief musician who is responsible for leading this musical praise. So, if corporate singing is going to be biblically administered, it requires a song leader. Song leaders are therefore ministering servants of God (*Elohiym* 430). Since He is King of all the earth, He deserves our musical worship. He also requires song leaders to minister with musical and spiritual understanding (*sakal* 7919).

The Hebrew word *sakal* means to be circumspect, intelligent, expert, to instruct or influence. It is the responsibility of the song leader to cause the worshipping body of Christ to understand that God is *Elohiym* (the exceeding God) and that the Lord is YHVH (the self-existent, eternal God who is), and that as King of all the earth, He is deity, worthy of adoration.

Song for the Day

Teach Me Thy Way, O Lord by B.M. Ramsey

Thought for the Day

Maybe the reason so many churches no longer employ a song leader is because so many church musicians use conducting gestures but fail to passionately lead others in worship.

Prayer for the Day

O Thou self-existent, eternal, living God, You are the supreme God, for You are not only the living God, but You are also the King of all the earth. Help me as a musician to cause the people to understand that You are worthy of all worship. Amen.

September 5

Elohim, the Supreme God, Helps Musicians

Psalm 49:1, 4— "To the chief Musician, A Psalm for the sons of Korah. Hear this, all ye people; give ear, all ye inhabitants of the world... I will incline mine ear to a parable: I will open my dark saying upon the harp."

It appears that this verse does not represent the chief musician speaking, but rather God, who declares that He will make known the mysteries of godliness using a musician playing a musical instrument. It is an incredible thought that God uses instrumental music as a vehicle to enhance the spiritual understanding of "all ye people" or "all ye inhabitants of the world."

God did not say that the music alone would open the people's mind to spiritual things, but in verses seven and eight that *Elohiym*(430), the supreme God, would redeem the soul. Somehow God, in His great wisdom, has chosen to use instrumental musicians to help accomplish His mighty purposes.

Song for the Day

Guide Me O Thou Great Jehovah by W. Williams

Thought for the Day

If the music part of music does not say anything, then we should not waste the worshippers' time by playing instrumental music.

Prayer for the Day

Thank You, Lord, for allowing instrumentalists to be of such great use in Your kingdom. Help all of us who lead or perform instrumental music to be useful in Your kingdom. Help us to always use instrumental music in a way that will bring glory to Your name. Thank You for Your great wisdom. Amen.

September 6

"Under God's Hands" for Ministry

I Chronicles 25:6 — "All these were under the hands of their father for song in the house of the Lord, with cymbals, psalteries, and harps, for the service of the house of God..."

The temple musicians were placed "under the hands of" the chief musicians Asaph, Jeduthun and Heman. This reference doubtlessly refers to the use of *cheironomy*. Cheironomers were musicians who used hand signs to represent pitches to be played by the temple musicians. It is significant that these Levite sons were under the "hands," i.e., direction, of spiritual men who had been "separated" (see 25:1) to serve YHVH through music. Why were these young Levite musicians being trained by the chief musicians? They were being prepared for service (*abodah* 5656) in the house of God.

The Bible lessons are clear here. It is the responsibility for church musicians to train our own to minister in the "house of God." It is part of every church musician's responsibility to train others to serve God by musicing unto Him. The Hebrew word *abodah* means to labor, minister or work, and it also connotes the idea of a bondservant. It is our responsibility to catechize our sons and daughters in the burden, responsibility and necessity of a continuing musical ministry from generation to generation.

Song for the Day

Give of Your Best to the Master by H.B. Grose

Thought for the Day

If we want the next generation to share our music values, we must be the ones who influence them musically.

Prayer for the Day

Lord, please help me to somehow impress upon the next generation of musicians the burden and responsibility of continued music ministry in the house of God. Help me to be a Godly mentor to the next generation of Christian musicians. I am asking You to increase my burden and passion for song like You did for Chenaniah. Amen.

September 7

The Songs of the LORD

I Chronicles 25:7 — "So the number of them, with their brethren that were instructed in the songs of the Lord, even all that were cunning, was two hundred fourscore and eight."

The chief musicians of the first Temple were responsible for the training of 288 musicians who would carry on the music ministry of the Temple. Asaph, Heman and Jeduthun were each responsible for training ninety-six musicians to carry on the music ministry of the church and Christian school. I wonder if it will be possible that ninety-six men and women will follow God's call into music ministry as a result of my influence.

Church musician, how many men and women are you mentoring to enter a music ministry? Are you more concerned about your programs, performances and personal musical performance skills than you are about those whom God has placed under your "hands"? Are you praying and doing everything you can to mentor young musicians to listen for the voice of YHVH who is still "separating" musicians to the service of the house of God?

Song for the Day

Lord, Be Glorified by B. Kilpatrick

Thought for the Day:

What will public worship be like forty years from now if your children grow up only liking the religious music you listen to and like?

Prayer for the Day

Lord, please help me not to consume the gifts and graces that You have given me upon my own lusts. Please help me to carry a spiritual burden for those musicians who work with me and under me. Make it possible that I will be able to influence the next generation of musicians to serve You through their musicing. Amen.

September 8

Peace with God

Romans 5:3-4— "…we glory in tribulations also: knowing that tribulation worketh patience; And patience, experience; and experience, hope…"

When things aren't going well, musicians often quote "tribulation worketh patience." However, I have never heard a Christian musician say, "I glory in tribulation." I know that I am not thrilled when I go through trials. Neither do I pray for patience, knowing full well that such a prayer might bring about a greater problem in my life!

The point St. Paul was making was not that we should ask for tribulation, but that the Christian has peace with God through Jesus Christ our Lord when he or she is surrounded with trouble. It is not always possible to see good in a situation while you are going through a trial, but a Christian knows that "…all things work together for good to them that love God, to them who are the called according to his purpose" (Romans 8:28).

As a Christian, we go through times of trouble, and when we do, it is important to remember that God cares about our everyday lives. Knowing this, we can have peace with God no matter what type of tribulation we face. This peace gives us a lively hope in God as we learn patience, gain experience, and greater hope in Jesus Christ our Lord.

Song for the Day

I Must Tell Jesus by Elisha Hoffman

Thought for the Day

Don't expect to be overjoyed when you are going through tribulation. During these times you will have to love and adore God on purpose.

Prayer for the Day

Lord, as I walk with You, I know that there will be times of trouble that come to me. Lord, please help me to have Your peace when I go through these tribulations. Help me to understand that You will use these troubles to draw me closer to You. Lord, help me to stay close to You no matter what I have to go through in this life. Help me to realize that You will make all these things work together for my good, and that You will never do anything to destroy my hope in You. These things I pray in Your loving name. Amen.

September 9

Relax, God Really did Create Music

Genesis 1:1 — "In the beginning God created the heaven and the earth."

Genesis 1:31 — "And God saw everything that He had made, and, behold, it was very good..."

In the beginning, there was God. In the beginning God created. In the beginning, God created music. How can you as a musician, know for sure that in the beginning, God created music? You can know it for sure because St. John 1:3 states that "all things were made by him; and without him was not anything made that was made."

Furthermore, I Corinthians 8:6 explains that "But to us there is but one God, the Father, of whom are all things, and we in him; and one Lord Jesus Christ, by whom are all things, and we by him." Paul also tells us in Colossians 1:16, "For by him were all things created, that are in heaven, and that are in earth, visible and invisible... all things were created by him, and for him."

So, relax. You don't have to worry about how music got started. God really did create music! These verses establish the fact that God created music. Therefore, He owns music since He created it in a very personal way. Music was created by God for His glory.

So, as a Christian musician you can relax, you are not philosophically responsible for the existence of music. You are merely His servant. Although you are a "king and a priest" unto God, all you have to do is to be obedient to His will, serve Him and honor Him with your musicing, mentor others musically, and instruct them in the "songs of the Lord" as you follow Bible principles of musicing unto God.

Song for the Day

How Great Thou Art by S.K. Kline

Thought for the Day

Stay on track musically. Remember, a train goes nowhere unless it is on track!

Prayer for the Day

Thank You, God, for creating music. Thank You for letting me minister musically unto You. Thank You for allowing me to minister your music unto You in the

Holy Place. Thank You for allowing me to mentor others musically and have a tiny part of their musical and spiritual development. Lord, I love You and I would do this all over again. Amen.

September 10

Ministering for God to His People

Romans 1:25— "They exchanged the truth about God for a lie, and worshiped and served created things rather than the Creator—who is forever praised. Amen. (NIV)

This passage is a discourse on the wrath of God against Roman idolatry. Verse 28 explains that these people "...did not retain God in their knowledge..." What was the result? "...God gave them over to a reprobate mind..." and they worshipped and served things rather than the Creator.

Music is a created thing. Christian music should never give homage and reverence to music. Too many Christian musicians live to perform music. Performance feeds their ego and fuels and empowers their lives. Music should not "keep a musician going." The power for service that the Holy Spirit gives to the Spirit-filled musician should cause their music ministry to be effective.

If a Christian is truly sold out to Christ, he or she will not live for performance but rather for Christ. The mature Christian musics for God's glory and the congregation's edification. The Spirit-led musician leads others in God-honoring musicing in the Holy Place. The mature Christian musician will seek to bring praise unto the blessed Father, Son and Holy Ghost rather than to self.

Song for the Day

The Wonder of It All by George B. Shea

Prayer for the Day

Lord, grant it that I will always music unto You instead of just the congregation. Protect me from the idolatry of worshipping music rather than worshipping You with music. Please don't let me exchange the truth of worshipping You for the lie of believing that I can worship Your creation. Amen.

September 11

Music Ministry—A Sacred Trust

II Chronicles 29:25— "And he set [*amad* 5975] the Levites in the house of the Lord with cymbals, with psalteries, and with harps, according to the commandment of David, and of Gad the king's seer, and Nathan the prophet: for so was the commandment of the LORD by his prophets."

Part of the process of Hezekiah's purification of the Temple was "setting" the music ministry in order. The Hebrew word *amad* connotes to confirm, to appoint, to employ or establish. The purification of Temple worship was not complete until the music ministry was established.

Although preaching of the Word is what the Bible calls the "power of God," music ministry is and has always been a concomitant of the expounding the Word of God in the Holy Place. If the music ministry in God's house is carried out by those who do not have a proper perspective of music's place in the context of worship, it will be tenuous and will often not be efficacious. Efficacious musicing has always been a necessity in the Holy Place.

Do you consider your musicing in the Holy Place to be a sacred trust? Do you consider that what you do as a church musician is done not only at the command of the pastor and the church board but also at the command of God? There is a vast philosophical and spiritual chasm between performing for your own aggrandizement and being truly a "priest" unto God with your musicing in the Holy Place.

Song for the Day

He is Lord, anonymous

Thought for the Day

Every time Israel refused to listen to God, they got into trouble.

Prayer for the Day

Lord, cleanse away all self and pride of perfection of performance in my musicing unto You. Teach me to truly minister unto You. Help me as a Christian musician to not only come under the pastor's authority but also under Your authority. Lord, teach me to be Your musical servant. Amen.

September 12

Praising the Lord Jehovah

Isaiah 12:2-5 — "Behold, God is my salvation; I will trust, and not be afraid: for the LORD JEHOVAH [3050 3068] is my strength and my song; he also is become my salvation. Therefore with joy shall ye draw water out of the wells of salvation. And in that day shall ye say, Praise the LORD, call upon his name, declare his doings among the people, make mention that his name is exalted. Sing unto the LORD; for he hath done excellent things: this is known in all the earth."

Isaiah prophesied of the coming, peaceable kingdom of Christ in chapter eleven. Chapter twelve is an admonition for Israel to praise the LORD for being Israel's strength, song and salvation. Jah-Jehovah means the vehement God who is the independent, eternal God who is. I am blessed when I think that Isaiah used two names to try to explain who God is. I am overwhelmed when I think of the forgiving, loving, merciful nature of God that is so expansive that one word would not explain what God meant to him.

His response was an admonition to praise, make supplication, testify, exalt, and last but not least, to sing. What is your response to this great God? As a Christian musician, I know that you sing and play for Him. I know that you are constantly drawing goodness out of the wells of salvation.

Do you draw help, deliverance and victory out of the wells of salvation with gladness, cheerfulness, joy and even mirth? Are you a "happy camper?" It is one thing to be a faithful musical servant but is another to be a happy, cheerful and joyful musical servant. Do you cry and shout for joy when you music unto the Holy One of Israel?

Be sure that when you sing of His high and exalted name that you do so with a heart full of joy because "he hath done excellent things: this is known in all the earth."

Song for the Day

He has Made Me Glad by Leona Brethorst

Prayer for the Day

Hallelujah! Lord, You have provided not only a well of salvation but a multiplicity of wells. Thank You for Your wells of goodness, mercy, forgiveness, protection, guidance, correction, instruction, love, longsuffering, wisdom, understanding and all the other wells I have needed or will need in the future. Help me to draw from them with joy and gladness all the days of my life. Amen.

September 13

Men who Desire to be Christ-like Musicians

Ephesians 5:25, 28 — "Husbands, love your wives, even as Christ also loved the church, and gave himself for it... So ought men to love their wives as their own bodies. He that loveth his wife loveth himself."

If you are a lady, you don't have to read this devotion today. If you are a man who is married or even remotely thinking about getting married—you must read this devotion.

Married men need to hear this admonition or the Holy Spirit would not have inspired the Ephesians writer to make such a statement. This wise writer stated in verse 29, "For no man ever yet hated his own flesh; but nourisheth and cherisheth it..."

Men are usually big babies when it comes to pain. One has said if men were to give birth to children, every family would only have one child! The Ephesians writer reminds us here that Christ gave himself for the church. That meant pain and suffering! Christ did not put Himself and His comfort above His love.

Men can often be emotional people, who tend toward selfishness and self-pity. This can cause them to expect to be babied by their wives. Part of being a Christ-like musician is loving your wife! Men, in the midst of your busy life give her all the attention you would give your thumb if you smashed it! Hold her close with tenderness. Give your wife some attention today! Love is not always an emotion; it is a choice. Find out what her love language is and feed that need. Do dishes, take out the trash, mop the kitchen or maybe really listen to her for once in your life!

Song for the Day

When Love is Found by B. Wren

Thought for the Day

Men, have you listened to your wife today?

Prayer for the Day

Lord, help me to love my wife more. Not for just what she can give to me, but help me to love her like I love my own body. Help me to put her ahead of myself today. Help me to know how to fulfill her needs. In your name I pray, Amen.

September 14

Hymning Unto God

Matthew 26:30— "And when they had sung an hymn, they went out into the mount of Olives."

Many of the Bible commentators tell us that the word hymn (*humneo* 5214) meant to sing a psalm. However, I'm not so sure, because St. Matthew knew about the word *psalmos*, which was the precise, Greek word for psalm. Also, St. Mark used the same word *psalmos* in Mark 14:26.

Christ sang or "hymned" with his disciples at the Last Supper. St. Luke wrote of the Eucharist, "...this do in remembrance of me." Is it farfetched that we should hymn unto Christ as a remembrance of Him?

If you as a church musician would treat hymning unto God as reverently as pastors treat the Lord's Supper, singing would take on a new dimension in your church. If you would make sure that your choir was as careful of the words they sing unto God as the words they pray unto God, maybe God's presence would fill the house as it did in the Temple (II Chronicles 5:12-14). If your church orchestra considers their musicing to be a prayer response to God, they would be careful not to play irreverently before the Holy One in the Holy Place.

We have found the musical enemy! It is us. Search your

heart, chief musician, to be sure that we are truly "hymning unto God." Remember that just like the Last Supper, Christ is in our midst when we sing or play a hymn. He has promised to inhabit our praise (Psalm 22:3).

Song for the Day

I Will Praise Him by M. J. Harris

Thought for the Day

When you remember God the Father, God the Son, and God the Holy Spirit through theologically accurate hymns and God-honoring instrumental music, it will make you, and the people you musically pastor, spiritually stronger.

Prayer for the Day

Forgive me, Lord, for not being more careful in my hymning unto You. Help me to be a genuine worship leader. Lord, help me to know how to lead others in musical worship. Help me to realize that if You considered it important to sing a hymn, then it is important that we hymn unto You today. Amen.

September 15

Children Training Musically Under Our Hands

I Chronicles 25:3 — "Of Jeduthun: the sons of Jeduthun; Gedaliah, and Zeri, and Jeshaiah, Hashabiah, and Mattithiah, six, under the hands of their father Jeduthun, who prophesied with a harp, to give thanks and to praise the LORD."

What a wonderful example of a God-like musician who instructed his own sons in the "songs of the LORD."(vs.7) These six sons were "under the hands" of their father. Praise God! What a wonderful example of a musician who took time for his own family's music education. He took the time necessary to train his own household. I Timothy 5:8 states, "But if any provide not for his own, and specially for those of his own house, he hath denied the faith, and is worse than an infidel."

I am amazed that some who love and serve Jesus Christ do not recognize the great need for the next generation to be "instructed in the songs of the LORD." Many parents who are not Christians are more consistent in training their children musically than Christian musicians. I have often told college music students who were in my music classes to "either train your children musically or hire a proxy."

One more concept is noteworthy in this passage of Scripture. Jeduthun prophesied (to sing by inspiration) with his harp. It was significant that he sang by inspiration, but it was just as important that he taught his six sons to prophesy with their musicing unto God. He taught his sons to give thanks, i.e., hold out their hands in avowal and thankfulness to God. He also taught them to praise (*halal* 1984) and to show or to boast of the self-existent, eternal God.

Are your children training musically under your hands? Are you personally mentoring them in how to music unto God? Are you teaching them by example how to praise and thank the Lord through music-making?

Song for the Day

All Things Bright and Beautiful by C.A. Alexander

Thought for the Day

How long has it been since you taught a child a worthwhile "song of the Lord"?

Prayer for the Day

Lord, help me to make music unto You. Help me to take time to train my children in how to praise and thank You with their musicing. Give me the strength and wisdom to train my own household in the songs of the Lord. Amen.

September 16

Singing to the Rock of Our Salvation

Psalm 95:1-2 — "Come, let us sing for joy to the LORD; let us shout aloud to the Rock of our salvation. Let us come before him with thanksgiving and extol him with music and song." (NIV)

Why do we sing unto the Lord? We sing because our hearts are joyful. We are so excited about Jesus the rock of our salvation that we shout aloud because of the thanksgiving and praise that wells up in our hearts. Because of this joy, we come before His presence with thanksgiving.

What does it mean to extol the Lord with our musicing? The word *ruwa* (7321) which is justly translated extol in the NIV means to shout aloud or to music with great strength. It does not connote noise making as the AV would suggest. The word *todah* (3034) which is translated thanksgiving means literally to extend the hands in worship. The words music, song and psalms are derived from the Hebrew word *zamiyr* (2158) which means to accompany a song with instrumental music. So when we extol God with songs accompanied by musical instruments, we music with great strength.

Because we joy in the presence of the LORD, we shout aloud the praises of the self-existent, eternal God who is. We enhance our praise music by singing with instrumental accompaniment. Because our God is worthy of praise, we lift our hands in avowal to the triune God.

Chief musician, is your heart full of mighty praises to our wonderful Lord? If not, remember that God is the rock of your salvation. As you remember who He is and what He has done, and what He is capable of doing, you can actually come into His presence with praiseful musicing.

Song for the Day

Holy Ground by Geron Davis

Thought for the Day

When you don't understand what God is doing in your life, make sure your heart is full of love and adoration toward Him.

Prayer for the Day

Lord, help me to be thankful for who You are and what You have done for me personally. You are the rock of my salvation. I want You to know that I love You, Lord. Help me to shout Your praises and sing with great acclamation about Your saving grace. These things I pray in Your name. Amen.

September 17

Led Away by Music

Nahum 2:7 — "And Huzzab shall be led away captive, she shall be brought up, and her maids shall lead her as with the voice of doves, tabering upon their breasts."

Although there is an argument surrounding the name Huzzab, it is thought by some scholars to be the name of the queen of Nineveh. The Book of Nahum records that Huzzab was led away captive by music. Verse seven states that her maids led her heart away by the use of beautiful, soothing or gentle use of music accompanied by breast drums. The meaning of the word *taphaph* (8608) is "to drum." These small drums consisted of a hoop covered with skin. These drums had a string attached which was looped around the maids' necks. They were played by the use of both hands tapping the heads of the drums.

Christian musicians often fear wild, loud, raucous, dissonant music sung and played by musicians wearing gaudy silver chains or performed by musicians adorned in tight leather pants, hobnailed boots and have their hair dyed bright purple. However, this Scripture gives an Old Testament example of one being led away captive with the sound of small breast drums accompanying maids with the "voice of doves." Those of us who are accustomed to the sounds that doves produce know that they create a soft, pleasing sound.

All music has power; and therefore, all styles of music exert power over the performer and the listener. So, the Christian musician must carefully consider this potential power that music will have when he or she musics in public or private. Music should edify the believer instead of drawing his or her heart away from God. Because music can lead us either away from our heavenly father or draw us closer to Him, we must carefully choose and utilize "style" when musicing unto God.

Song for the Day

When in Our Music God is Glorified by Fred Pratt Green

Thought for the Day

It is a novel idea to many Christian musicians that music has the propensity to help or to hinder public worship. Since it does have great power, musicians must choose content, style, and performance praxis very carefully.

September 18

Acknowledging that God Owns what He Created (Part 1)

Colossians 1:16 — "For by him were all things created, that are in heaven, and that are in earth..."

Most Christian musicians do not have any trouble believing that God created. As a matter of fact, many of them believe that He created things that are in the heavens and things that are on or in the earth. However, some musicians get nervous when one considers that God created music. You see, He did create music because music is part of "all" of His creation. It is not that these musicians doubt His creation. However, they sort of believe that God made music, and that man also makes music.

If one has the notion that man created music, or that he created anything for that matter, this musician has a faulty view of creation and music's beginning. If man created music, then he owns it because man took nothing and made something—music. However, only God is capable of taking nothing and making something out of what did not exist.

So, the purpose of this little discussion today is to give Christians a clear philosophical view of the fine art that they use to worship God. Every Christian musician must realize that he or she merely takes God's musical building blocks, i.e., the elements of music, and arranges them in an order which we call musical compositions. Therefore we, as Christian musicians, are only the "handmaidens" of God's great creation we call music. Furthermore, our heavenly Father has entrusted us to be stewards, not owners, of his creation we call music.

Song for the Day

Immortal, Invisible, God Only Wise by Walter C. Smith

Thought for the Day

A part of a Christian musician's total surrender to Jesus Christ our Lord and Savior is acknowledging God's ownership of the great art of music.

September 19

Acknowledging that God Owns what He Created (Part 2)

Colossians 1:16— "For by him were all things created, that are in heaven, and that are in earth, visible and invisible…"

Yesterday we learned that the "all" of God's creation includes music. Today we learn that God's creation includes the visible (*horatos* 3707) and the invisible (*aoratos* 517). The word *horatos* which is used here is a *hapax legomenon*, is the visible part that we can see on the musical score. The *aoratos* is the part of a musical composition that we cannot see when we look at the musical score.

The invisible part of music is sound. As Christian musicians, we are responsible to God for the visible part of the music and the invisible part of the music. In other words, we are responsible to God, not only for the words and notes we place on the musical score, but also the vocal and instrumental sounds that we produce when we music unto our heavenly Father.

Therefore, the sounds that you produce and the sounds that the musicians produce who work under your musical direction, all come under the direct lordship of Jesus Christ. When you face Him "who hath his eyes like unto a flame of fire" (Revelation 2:18) in the Day of Judgment, you will give an account for the sounds that you and your vocal, choral and instrumental groups musiced unto God.

Prayer for the Day

Lord, I know that You understand sound and care about sounds, because You created the mechanisms that make sounds possible. Please help me to produce musical sounds that will bring honor and glory unto You. Please help me to be able to discern the difference in which sounds are properly to be produced for the awesomeness and solemnity of worshipping the triune God. Please give me the spiritual and musical discernment to tell the difference between the sacred and the profane. These things I pray in Your awesome name. Amen.

Song for the Day

When in Our Music God is Glorified by Fred Pratt Green

September 20

Acknowledging that God Owns what He Created (Part 3)

Colossians 1:17-18— "And he is before all things, and by him all things consist. And he is the head of the body, the church: who is the beginning, the firstborn from the dead; that in all things he might have the preeminence."

The last two days have laid a foundation for the Christian to music within the framework of Colossians 1:17. So, today we will learn that in all our musicing Christ must have the preeminence. The farmers would say back in Kansas, "You have to share the pig." However, I contend that we, as "sold out to Christ" musicians, must give Christ the entire "pig."

It is impossible for Christ to have the preeminence in your musicing unless He owns all of your music and all of your musicing unto God. Unless you have submitted all your musicing unto the lordship of Jesus Christ, God does not completely own music in your life and ministry.

Remember that the religious humanist believes that his or her musicing is for the performer's aggrandizement and the seeker's enjoyment. To the religious, humanist church musician, church music is about the likes and dislikes of the musician and the seeker. To this musician's thinking, Christ will be happy with whatever the seeker and the seeker's servant (the church musician) likes.

Prayer for the Day

Lord, please help me not to get sucked into the humanistic vacuum of political correctness when it comes to musicing unto You. Please help me to present the gospel of Christ in a way that the seeker will understand the musical gospel message and at the same time bring honor to the Triune God we love and serve. Help me to always give Christ the preeminence in all my musicing. This I am asking in Your wise name. Amen.

September 21

Christian Musicing is Like a Light

Matthew 5:16 — "Let your light so shine before men, that they may see your good works, and glorify your Father which is in heaven."

The light of Christ placed in us is so powerful that Satan needs a bushel basket to completely hide it from those who see it and will receive its light in their lives. Satan knows that, without this light of Christ, people will continue to live in darkness. Jesus instructed us to put our powerful light on a candlestick, so that it will give the light of salvation to all people.

One of the ways that a Christian can show the light of Christ is through his or her musicing. Jesus explained in this sermon, that "you" are the light of the world. This means that there is much value in people seeing the Christian musician music unto God. As I play exegetical gymnastics with this verse of Scripture, I have the notion that maybe Jesus includes our musicing unto Him as a part of what people need to "see." If so, musicians need to let their musical light shine in such a way that all will see it and glorify our Father who is in heaven. Therefore, we need to be very careful of what people "see" as well as what they hear when we music unto God. God is the provider of the light, but we are His musical candles.

Song for the Day

The Light of the World is Jesus by Philip P. Bliss

Thought for the Day

If musicing unto God is a part of our good works, and it is, then Christian musicians need to be sure that people see and hear good quality music when we sing and play in and out of church.

September 22

Many Shall see Your Musicing

Psalm 40:3 — "And he hath put a new song in my mouth, even praise unto our God: many shall see it, and fear, and shall trust in the LORD."

This Psalm confirms that part of music's ability to accomplish its mission is the fact that people can see it happen. We, as Christian musicians, are most often interested in people hearing our musicing unto God. Today we are going to consider, for just a moment, that "many shall see" our new song, of a higher renovated character, which is "praise unto our God."

What is the importance of people seeing us music unto God? When we place our musicing on a candlestick (see yesterday's discussion) many people see us present a musical offering unto Him. The Bible doesn't say that it is important that people like our musical offering, but rather it states very clearly that it is seeing our musicing unto God that causes them to fear God. So, as people see us music unto God it can cause them to fear God through the convicting power of the Holy Spirit. However, it is the saving power of Jesus Christ which will cause them to trust in the LORD.

Song for the Day

Open Our Eyes by Robert Cull

Thought for the Day

Have you ever thought about what you look like when you music unto God? As a Christian musician you should, based on today's Scripture lesson, be very careful what the audience sees when you are musicing to the God you love and serve with joy.

September 23

Be Ready to Fall Down

Daniel 3:5 — "That at what time ye hear the sound of the cornet, flute, harp, sackbut, psaltery, dulcimer, and all kinds of musick, ye fall down and worship the golden image that Nebuchadnezzar the king hath set up."

This ancient description sounds like a twenty-first century admonition to worship whenever and whatever is "going down" musically at a particular time. These three Hebrew men refused to violate their consciences musically or spiritually. Twenty-first century musicians are at times put in a place where they will have to take a stand. The Bible lesson in this Scripture is very clear. These three men would not worship the Chaldean image and they would not worship with "all kinds of music."

The result was that they got themselves thrown into a fiery furnace. Sorry! These men took a stand about worship style and idol worship which incurred the wrath of those who were in charge. Those in authority were so mad that they heated the furnace seven times hotter than normal. So, if you take a stand musically and spiritually, get ready to enter the fiery furnace

These three Hebrew men maintained a meek and quiet spirit, which included a good attitude, and God honored them and took care of them. You may feel that you are in the fiery furnace because you refuse to go along with worship that does not follow Bible principles of musicing unto God. However, you must stay "cool" in the midst of the hot furnace. If you do, God will take care of you. He cared so much for Shadrach, Meshach, and Abednego that God got in the furnace with them.

Thought for the Day

Sometimes twenty-first century Christian musicians believe that they are the first musicians to find themselves in the middle of the fiery furnace of a worship war. However, the Bible records a worship war going on in ancient times at the court of King Nebuchadnezzar.

September 24

More on Good and Faithful Musicians (Part 1)

Matthew 25:21— "His lord said unto him, Well done, thou good and faithful servant: thou hast been faithful over a few things, I will make thee ruler over many things: enter thou into the joy of thy lord."

A musician can be a good servant morally and not be passionately faithful to the responsibilities of the music ministry where God has placed that musician. Christian character is what makes a musician a good (*agathos* 18) person. The word *agathos* means good in any sense, but its meaning is different than the word *pistos* (4103) which means objectively "trustworthy," i.e., in the case of a Christian musician, one who experiences the actual reality of being a completely trustworthy servant musician of Christ.

It stands to reason that moral goodness is a necessary requirement of the ministering musician who is a bondservant (*doulos* 1401) of our Lord and Savior Jesus Christ. Ralph Earle stated that "these are the only two things

God requires of everyone—that he be good in character and faithful in service."[1] Although God requires both, I do not believe that being a morally good person automatically makes one a quality musician or does it make one a faithful, trustworthy, passionate music leader.

Quote for the Day

Lenski states, "The master (lord), who is a type of Christ, pronounces this verdict on his servant, 'Slave excellent and reliable!' and thus furnishing his master great satisfaction. No higher commendation can come to any believer from the lips of Jesus."[2]

September 25

More on Good and Faithful Musicians (Part 2)

Matthew 25:21— "His lord said unto him, Well done, thou good and faithful servant: thou hast been faithful over a few things, I will make thee ruler over many things: enter thou into the joy of thy lord."

A part of being a faithful musical servant is learning how to use music as a worship vehicle. Even if a musician loves music and is passionate about performing it, he or she is not necessarily a faithful musical servant. There is a vast difference between loving music so much that one worships it and loving God so much that one has a great passion for using music as a concomitant to worshipping the God who created it. As we all know, the Bible condemns worshipping created things (see Romans 1:25). The faithful musical servant leads others in worship and at the same time worships God through the music he or she is using as a worship vehicle.

The faithful musical servant is not only a leader and a worshipper but also a faithful teacher. Faithful musical leadership includes teaching others to worship God by musicing unto Him. The faithful musical servant utilizes teaching skills in their most profound form, i.e., teaching by example. The faithful musical servant is not only a technical leader but also an anointed servant.

Starting late in the twentieth century Christian writers and music philosophers began to make acrid comments about those who sought the anointing of the Holy Spirit as though such philosophical belief was egotistical or somewhat fanatical. Although it may not be a popular concept among Christians in this century, the visitation of God upon human servants is certainly a Biblical concept. For examples, see Leviticus 7:35, 8:12; 1 Samuel 15:1; Isaiah 10:27; James 5:14; and 1 John 2:27.

Quote for the Day

This quote is found in the Broadband Bible Commentary: "Faithfulness over a little opens the way for one to be entrusted with much. The reward for faithful service is also known in terms of entry into the joy of one's master."[3]

September 26

More on Good and Faithful Musicians (Part 3)

Ephesians 5:18-19 — "And be not drunk with wine, wherein is excess; but be filled with the Spirit; Speaking to yourselves in psalms and hymns and spiritual songs, singing and making melody in your heart to the Lord."

I strongly believe that the good and faithful musical leader should and must be moved deeply by the message of the music that is being used as a worship vehicle. It is one thing to be moved intellectually by the meaning of the music, but it is another to have the *dunamis* (1411) of the Spirit, which comes only to good and faithful Spirit-filled musical servants.

Many Christian musicians seem to forget that the great musical discourse in the fifth chapter of Paul's epistle to the Ephesians, not only includes verse nineteen, but also verse eighteen that states, "And be not drunk with wine, wherein is excess; but be filled with the Spirit." What is taught in verse nineteen can only happen to those who are living a life in the Spirit. Verse eighteen teaches a continual life in the Spirit after the Christian is once filled. The good and faithful musical servant that is spoken of in the fifth chapter of Ephesians is also admonished to let the Holy Spirit have control of his or her life and music ministry.

The influence of the Divine upon the human can and should be a reality in the twenty-first century. The musician who is touched and moved by the Holy Spirit has the right to be passionate about the music that he or she uses as a vehicle of worship. All of the accomplished Christian musicians that I have had the privilege to know have been very passionate about their secular musicing. However, some of them believe that their sacred musicing should be very sedate and staid and should be executed in a manner that is seemingly almost detached from any passion or emotion. I see no place in Scripture where Christian musicians are instructed to perform sacred music in a manner that is devoid of outward emotion, outward evidence of meaning (understanding), or outward physical expression of being passionate about the music being performed. Therefore, I am drawn to the philosophical conclusion that although sacred musicing is very serious business, we may and should perform it with joy.

Quote for the Day

"One hallmark of the Spirit's filling will be a desire to give vocal expression to the heart's devotion *to the Lord* by the use of canticles and songs which the Spirit inspires."[4]

September 27

More on Good and Faithful Musicians (Part 4)

Nehemiah 8:10— "Then he said unto them, Go your way, eat the fat, and drink the sweet, and send portions unto them for whom nothing is prepared: for this day is holy unto our LORD: neither be ye sorry; for the joy of the LORD is your strength."

Psalm 89:15 states, "Blessed is the people that know the joyful sound [*teruah* 8643—great acclamation of joy]: they shall walk, O LORD, in the light of thy countenance." Psalm 149:1-2, "Praise ye the LORD. Sing unto the LORD a new song, and his praise in the congregation of saints. Let Israel rejoice in him that made him: let the children of Zion be joyful [*giyl*, 1523] in their King." The word *giyl* is used in a great variety of applications in the Old Testament but it most often connotes gladness and rejoicing. These are only a few of the multitude of Scriptures that teach worshipping with much joy.

Certainly the fact that the Bible repeatedly mentions singing with joy should encourage us to music with outward joy and emotion. 1 Chronicles 15:16 states, "And David spake to the chief of the Levites to appoint their brethren to be the singers with instruments of musick, psalteries and harps and cymbals, sounding, by lifting up the voice with joy [*simchah*, 8057-exceeding gladness and pleasure]." Isaiah 12:2-3 states, "Behold, God is my salvation; I will trust, and not be afraid: for the LORD JEHOVAH is my strength and my song; he also is become my salvation. Therefore with joy [*sasown*, 8342—cheerfulness, gladness and mirth] shall ye draw water out of the wells of salvation." Zephaniah 3:17 states, "The Lord thy God in the midst of thee is mighty; he will save, he will rejoice over thee with joy; he will rest in his love, he will joy [*giyl*, see above] over thee with singing [*rinnah*, 7440—singing with gladness and joy]."

Sacred musical performance that has been devoid of the characteristics mentioned above has been one of the reasons that so many Christian musicians are becoming disillusioned with traditional sacred music. One of the other reasons has been that some busy musicians have failed to seek the aid and anointing of the Holy Spirit upon their sacred musicing. Therefore, I contend that a part of being a faithful servant is being completely submissive to the leadership of the Holy Spirit. Furthermore, a part of faithful musical servanthood involves being as passionate, and being even more passionate, about sacred musicing than one is about secular musicing.

Quote for the Day

"The importance of song as attracting to the House of God, as *interesting and spiritually benefiting* those engaged in worship, and as finding *audible expression* for devout feeling, should be fully enforced. It, therefore, becomes the duty of all who have the gift to lay it on the altar of God's service in the sanctuary."[5]

September 28

What a Friend We Have in Jesus

Proverbs 18:24 — "A man that hath friends must shew himself friendly: and there is a friend that sticketh closer than a brother."

Joseph Scriven's nineteenth-century hymn is many times published in standard hymnals with only the first three verses. The first verse introduces the hymn's prayer theme by establishing that it is truly a privilege to take everything to our God through prayer.

What a friend we have in Jesus,
All our sins and griefs to bear!

What a privilege to carry
Everything to God in prayer!
Oh, what peace we often forfeit,
Oh, what needless pain we bear,
All because we do not carry,
Everything to God in prayer!

The second verse teaches that we should not let life's troubles discourage us, because we are able to take our weaknesses, trials and temptations to our faithful friend Jesus.

Have we trials and temptations?
Is there trouble anywhere?
We should never be discouraged—
Take it to the Lord in prayer.
Can we find a friend so faithful,
Who will all our sorrows share?
Jesus knows our every weakness;
Take it to the Lord in prayer.

The third verse reminds us that when we are weak, heavy-laden, and even forsaken by our earthly friends, our precious Savior will take us in His arms where we may find solace.

Are we weak and heavy-laden?
Cumbered with a load of care?
Precious Savior, still our refuge—
Take it to the Lord in prayer.
Do thy friends despise, forsake thee?
Take it to the Lord in prayer!
In His arms He'll take and shield thee,
Thou wilt find a solace there.

The fourth verse adds a wonderful final dimension to this hymn. It reminds us that, as Hebrews 4:15 teaches, we do not have to bear our burdens alone, "For we have not an high priest which cannot be touched with the feeling of our infirmities; but was in all points tempted like as we are, yet without sin." It also teaches that, as James 5:16 says, "...The effectual fervent prayer of a righteous man availeth much." Finally, this verse states that the Christian will soon be in the presence of our Lord, where prayer will be replaced with endless worship. Praise God for this last verse which should always be included when we sing this prayer hymn. Read it and rejoice!

> Blessed Savior, Thou hast promised
> Thou wilt all our burdens bear;
> May we ever, Lord, be bringing
> All to Thee in earnest prayer.
> Soon in glory bright, unclouded,
> There will be no need for prayer—
> Rapture, praise, and endless worship
> Will be our sweet portion there.
>
> —JOSEPH M. SCRIVEN (1855)

Thought for the Day

Although sometimes prayer is not a time of sweetness but rather a titanic struggle, it is still a privilege to come to God in prayer.

Prayer for the Day

I want to thank You, precious Savior, that You are truly my friend. Thank You that You are always bigger than my troubles. I also want to thank You for the privilege of coming to You in prayer. In the time of trouble and temptation, I can always come to You, our sinless Savior, for help. Even if my earthly friends were to forsake me, You are a friend that will stick closer than a brother. Lord, help me to draw close to You so that You can take me up in Your strong arms and shield me from life's stormy blasts. Thank You for being such a wonderful Savior and friend. Amen.

September 29

Trusting God During Misunderstanding

Lamentations 3:14— "I was a derision to all my people; and their song all the day."

It is rewarding when others sing your compositions, but it is another thing when they make fun of you with their musicing. In his Lamentations, Jeremiah, in verse one of chapter three, recounted that "I am the man that hath seen affliction by the rod of his wrath." One must read the complete chapter or it will appear that Jeremiah was completely negative. However, in verse twenty-two he states, "It is of the LORD's mercies that we are not consumed, because his compassions fail not."

If you take a stand musically, you are probably going to be made fun of by others. This derision may come from those that are close enough to you to hurt you deeply. The only musicians that I know that are not misunderstood at times are those who are not doing anything for the Lord musically. So, get prepared to be misunderstood and at the same time get prepared to understand that the Lord will not let you be "consumed." The Psalmist put it this way in Psalm 121:2, which is one of the songs of ascents, "My help cometh from the LORD, which made heaven and earth." Since the creator of the universe desires to help you, let Him do it when you are misunderstood.

Song for the Day

Trust and Obey by John H. Sammis

Scripture for the Day

"For we have not an high priest which cannot be touched with the feeling of our infirmities; but was in all points tempted like as we are, yet without sin" (Hebrews 4:15).

Prayer for the Day

Lord, I know in my head that You are my source of help during the times that I am misunderstood, but help me to believe it in my heart. Help me to trust that You not only can help me, but that You will help me! During the times of misunderstanding, help me to not lean on my understanding, but to trust You like a little child trusts his earthly father. Lord, thank You for what You have done for me and what You will do in the future. These things I am praying in Your wonderful name. Amen.

September 30

The Noise of Your Songs

Amos 5:23 — "Take thou away from me the noise of thy songs; for I will not hear the melody of thy viols."

At the time that this Scripture was penned by the prophet Amos, Israel's heart was not right with God. So God spoke through Joel to tell Israel that He would not accept their meat offerings, thank offerings or their musical offerings. Because of Israel's "heart condition," God called their songs and their singing with instruments "noise." The Hebrew word rendered "noise" is *hamown* (1995) which means "a noise or a tumult."

Church musicians need to tune their hearts before they tune their harps. It was so in the days of the prophet Amos, and it is still true today. Our hearts must be in tune with God or our music is nothing more than noise to our God. Your taking time to read and study God's Word is just as important as organizing and practicing the music for Sunday morning worship! If you take time to read, pray and get your heart in tune with God, you will not be apt to hear God say, "I hate, I despise your feast days... Though ye offer me burnt offerings and your meat offerings, I will not accept them..." (Amos 5:21-22).

I have always told my students that the God of performance is also the God of rehearsal. If you come to rehearsal with your heart in tune with God, and if you "practice the presence of God" in rehearsals, you will never have to "put on" or act like you are enjoying God's presence when you give God a musical offering in a church service.

Thought for the Day

Christian musicians should always remember to be as careful in "tuning" their hearts as they are in tuning their instruments and singing in tune.

Endnotes:

1. A.F. Harper, ed., *Matthew-Luke*, vol. 6 in *Beacon Bible Commentary*, (Beacon Hill Press, 1965), 237.

2. R.C.H. Lenski, *Interpretation of St. Matthew's Gospel*, (Peabody, Mass: Hendrickson, 1998), 979.

3. Clifton J. Allen, *Matthew-Mark*, vol. 8 in *The Broadman Bible Commentary* (Nashville, Tennessee: Broadman Press, 1973), 225.

4. Clifton J. Allen, *II Corinthians-Philemon*, vol. 11, 166.

5. H.D.M. Spence-Jones, et al., *I Chronicles*, vol. 13 in *The Pulpit Commentary*, (Mclean, Va: MacDonald, 1980), 95.

OCTOBER

October 1

Keeping Musical Meditations "Sweet" (Part 1)

Psalm 104:33-34 — "I will sing unto the LORD as long as I live: I will sing praise to my God while I have my being. My meditation of him shall be sweet: I will be glad in the LORD."

This psalmist takes the responsibility to remain glad and to be sure that his musical meditations stay sweet. We do not know who this psalmist was, but he purposed in his heart to have control over his emotions. Verse thirty-three explains that he will travel around and sing, and play (*zamar* 2167), i.e., to touch or play a stringed instrument, and celebrate JHVH. He was declaring that he would on purpose sing and play the praises unto the LORD with a glad heart.

Furthermore, he purposed to keep his musical praises sweet (*areb* 6149), i.e., with pleasantness or pleasure. If there is anything that a church should experience, it is to observe a musician who sings and plays the high praises of God with great pleasure. Certainly, they should not have to endure a musical performance by a Christian musician who looks like he or she has just eaten an unusually sour lemon.

This psalmist pledged to sing and play with pleasure as long as he lived. It is worth noticing that this determined psalmist fully understood that the source of his gladness was God and not music or musical performance. This musical discourse makes it very clear that although this musician enjoyed singing and playing a stringed instrument, he purposed to worship God — not music.

Prayer for the Day

I want to thank You, LORD, for the gift of music. I also want to thank You that, in Your great wisdom, You created the great art form called music so that we can have another means of communicating with You. Please help me to always music unto You with great gladness. These things I am praying in Your name. Amen.

Song for the Day

I Will Sing of My Redeemer by Philip P. Bliss

Thought for the Day

After reading Psalm 104:33-34, I believe that Christian musicians never get to retire from joyful musicing unto God.

October 2

Keeping Musical Meditations "Sweet" (Part 2)

Psalm 104:33-34— "I will sing unto the LORD as long as I live: I will sing praise to my God while I have my being. My meditation of him shall be sweet: I will be glad in the LORD."

Christian musicians are emotional people who experience moments of extreme joy but are also prone to times of great depression. Many times during a musical presentation they soar to great emotional heights, and after the adrenalin ceases to flow, the bottom falls out emotionally and they find themselves in John Bunyan's "slough of despond."

This anonymous psalmist gave Christian musicians the formula for victorious musicing and living. He testified in the first person, "I will." This statement declares that he would not allow himself and his musicing to be controlled by his emotions. Rather than erroneously believe that emotions dictate how one musics unto God, he refused to let his emotional state of mind dictate when he would music unto God with joy, sweetness and gladness. He accomplished this by looking unto God for strength and gladness.

We know this because verse thirty-four declares, "I will

be glad in the LORD." Have you purposed in your heart to be glad when you music unto the Lord? Have you asked our great and wonderful God to help you get above the things that rob you of your joy?

Prayer for the Day

Heavenly Father, I am asking You to help me to be a proactive Christian musician. Help me to place my will in Your all-wise and wonderful control. I am looking to You as the source of my strength and gladness. Help me never to get sour, but rather to keep my musicing sweet and joyful. Please give me the wisdom to let You help me to control my emotions. These things I pray in Your all-wise and loving name. Amen.

Song for the Day

Joyful, Joyful, We Adore Thee by Henry van Dyke

Thought for the Day

When I couldn't seem to get my college choir to music with joy, I would sing this little song to them:
If you're happy and you know it—show your face.
If you're happy and you know it—show your face.
If you're happy and you know it—then your face
will surely show it.
So, if you're happy and you know it—show your
face.

October 3

Musicians in Perpetuity

1 Chronicles 25:6 — "All these were under the hands of their father for song in the house of the Lord, with cymbals, psalteries, and harps, for the service of the house of God, according to the king's order to Asaph, Jeduthun, and Heman."

Have you ever wondered why the level of music worship developed to such an advanced level during the time of the first and second Temples? When I was a Bible College divisional chair, some of the largest churches in Cincinnati would call me because they did not have accompanists to meet their ministry needs. They had money, facilities, and equipment, but they did not have musicians in perpetuity. They had planned and prepared for future ministries, but they had not accepted the responsibility to train their own church musicians.

1 Chronicles 25:7 explains that the Levite musicians who were in charge of the music of the ancient Jewish Temple trained musicians in perpetuity when it states, "So the number of them, with their brethren that were instructed in the songs of the LORD, even all that were cunning, was two hundred fourscore and eight." Many churches and Christian elementary and secondary schools do not even include music education in their church education program or their school academic curriculum. They seem not to consider music education to be a priority. Therefore, it is of little wonder that they do not have enough qualified musicians to meet the music needs of their ministry. Also, they do not realize that failure to educate students musically will result in a shortage of adult musicians that understand sacred musicing. As I have said many times, Christians cannot expect secular music educators to make sacred music a music education priority.

Chapter twenty-five of I Chronicles states clearly that they instructed (*lamad* 3925, i.e., they instructed, taught, made expert), or made to be skillful, all of their Levite musician sons. Can you imagine these God-fearing chief Levite teachers sending their sons to the Philistines, Amalekites, Jebusites, or Hivites to receive their musical training? It would have been the last thing on earth that would have entered into their thinking. These ancient musicians understood the importance of making a God-fearing music education a preferred claim on the musical activities of the Temple.

Because sacred music education was important to them, they taught their Levite sons personally. 1 Chronicles 25:1-2 explains,

> "Moreover David and the captains of the host separated to the service of the sons of Asaph, and of Heman, and of Jeduthun, who should prophesy with harps, with psalteries, and with cymbals: and the number of the workmen according to their service was: Of the sons of Asaph; Zaccur, and Joseph, and Nethaniah, and Asarelah, the sons of Asaph under the hands of Asaph, which prophesied according to the order of the king."

This passage explains that the musical sons of Asaph were educated by their father, i.e. "under the hands of" (*yad Asaph*, 3027 623). This statement connotes that these musicians were taught by the chief Levite Asaph. The same statement is made of Heman in verse six and Jeduthun in verse three. The Bible principal of music education is very clear. All of these chief Temple musicians considered the music education so important that they made it a priority.

Scripture for the Day

"And his mercy *is* on them that fear him from generation to generation" (Luke 1:50).

October 4

Those Who are "Under Your Hands"

I Chronicles 25:6— "All these were under the hands of their father for song in the house of the Lord, with cymbals, psalteries, and harps, for the service of the house of God, according to the king's order to Asaph, Jeduthun, and Heman."

The Levite sons were under their father's "hands for song" (*yad* shiyr 3027, 7891). This Scripture is a reference to *cheironomy*, i.e., the use of hand signs to designate pitches to the Levite musicians. So, these musicians were literally under the hands of their father, who was a cheironomer. Now centuries later, young people are under our hands for song like the Levite sons in ancient Israel. The conducting gestures used by the conductor actually place these ministering Christian musicians under the hands of the conductor.

It is an awesome responsibility to have children, young people, and adults who are depending on us for musical and spiritual leadership. Chapter twenty-five of I Chronicles is a discourse about the chief musicians who were music directors, and the young musicians who received musical training and leadership from godly musicians like Asaph, Heman (Ethan), and Jeduthun. These Levite men taught musical matters in the service of Elohim the supreme, exceeding God.

As a ministering musician, you have an awesome responsibility, like Heman, to be the King's "seer" or a beholder of a vision of God's kingdom (see I Chronicles 25:5). It is your responsibility to pass that vision on to those you minister with and those who are "under your hands."

Song for the Day

I Have Decided to Follow Jesus, anonymous

Thought for the Day

Are you mentoring any young musicians or are you consuming music on your own desires?

Prayer for the Day

Lord, I am "under Your hands" for song, and I realize that You have placed others "under my hands" to teach them to minister the vision to Your church. Please help me to catch a greater vision of You so that I may truly be a "seer" of spiritual things. Lord, may my life's vision be to bring glory to Your name through the use of music. These things I pray in Your name. Amen.

October 5

Musicing the Word of the Holy One of Israel

Psalm 71:22 — "I will also praise thee with the psaltery, even thy truth, O my God: unto thee will I sing with the harp, O thou Holy One of Israel."

The God worthy of our musical worship is *Elohiym* (430, the supreme plural form of the word for the exceeding God). The God who Israel worshipped with the harp and lyre in vocal and instrumental praise is identified as the "Holy One of Israel." The Hebrew words *qadosh Yisra'el* (6918, 3478) mean the only true God who is morally perfect or clean. This holy, supreme God must be worshipped in His "truth." Our musicing proclaims the "true" truth of our holy, supreme, exceeding God.

The psalmist was not only interested in singing and playing the hand-held lyre, but he was also concerned with proclaiming the absolute truth of God's message to His people. For a Christian musician to convincingly music the true truth of the Bible, he or she must believe that it is the absolute, accurate, inspired Word of God. A sincere Christian musician cannot honestly or efficaciously music what he or she does not believe. St. John 1:1 very clearly proclaims that "in the beginning was the Word, and the Word was with God, and the Word was God." As we know, the word *logos* (3056) means something said and all the divine expressions or accounts were breathed out by God. Therefore, God and what He has said in Scripture cannot be separated.

Every Christian musician must realize his or her musicing is important. As Christian musicians, we have the awesome opportunity and responsibility to sing and play about God's wonderful works, salvation and holiness. Twenty-first century Christian musicians must not get so busy performing that they forget that they are presenting the true truth of the "Holy One of Israel."

Thought for the Day

If God's Word is not true, then it is not worth musicing. If it is true, and it most certainly is, it is the most important part of a Christian's musicing.

October 6

Reading (Singing) Distinctly Gave the "Sense"

Nehemiah 8:8 — "So they read [intoned] in the book in the law of God distinctly, and gave the sense, and caused them to understand the reading."

This passage of Scripture has troubled many Bible expositors for centuries. They have often queried, "What made the reading of the scrolls of the Law 'distinct'?" They have also wondered how the Levite musicians were able to "give the sense" of the meaning of the Law? It has also been a great mystery as to what type or rendering of the scrolls by the Levite musicians actually took place. (We know from verse seven that the Levites were among those who "…caused the people to understand the law…")

This passage of Scripture, which over the many centuries has become esoteric, is a reference to the intoning or singing of the Law by the use of the *te'amim,* which is the biblical musical notation found above and below the Masoretic Text of the Hebrew Bible [*Tanakh*]. This intoning, cantillation or singing is what made the Levite rendering of the Law "distinct," i.e., more understandable to the people.

Note that the Bible does not say that the Levite musicians gave commentary (like the *Halakah* and *Haggadah* from the *Midrash*) on the content of the scrolls, but merely that their type of "reading," which refers to the singing of the Law through the use of the *te'amim*. We know with certainty that this rendering was performed so distinctly (*parash* 6567, i.e., to separate or to specify) that it gave specificity to the meaning of the text, so that the congregation understood the reading of the Torah.

So, you may legitimately ask, What should we learn from this text in the Book of Nehemiah? Christian musicians in the twenty-first century need to be acutely aware that proper, musical rendering of the good news of the Bible is absolutely essential. The music minister must render sacred music in such a way that the modern-day worshipper will be aware of the "sense" of the message in order to understand it distinctly. Proper musical rendering of the texts of the Bible has a hermeneutic function in that it helps to support and complete the meaning of the text.

Quote for the Day

"The Talmud says that the Bible should be read in public and be made understood to the hearers in sweet, musical tune. And he who reads the Pentateuch without tune shows disregard for it and the vital value of its laws. A deep understanding can be achieved only by singing the Torah… and whoever intones the Holy Scriptures in the manner of secular SONG abuses the Torah."[1]

Prayer for the Day

I want to thank You, my heavenly Father, for loving mankind enough to give us Your Word. Please help me to be able to music Your Word distinctly. Please give me more understanding of how I can effectively minister Your Word with music. Help me to cause others to have a deep understanding of Your Word. I am asking in Your wise and wonderful name. Amen.

October 7

Old Testament Priests Sounded an Alarm

Joel 2:1 — "Blow ye the trumpet in Zion, and sound an alarm in my holy mountain: let all the inhabitants of the land tremble: for the day of the LORD cometh, for it is nigh at hand."

The prophet Joel commanded the priests to blow an alarm with the shofar (7782), which was a ram's horn. The sounding of pitches from this powerful instrument, although it was not considered a melodic musical instrument because of the limited number of pitches it could produce, was used to sound an alarm for the people of Israel to hear. All assemblies of the children of Israel were signaled by the pitches produced on the shofar. On this particular occasion, the message of the prophet was that the day of judgment or punishment was about to happen.

Church musicians have no less responsibility in the twenty-first century. They are set apart by God to be "kings and priests" unto God (Revelation 1:6) to sound out the message of God's love and judgment. All Christian musicians have the responsibility to sound out the wonderful message because God has said that, "I will pour out my Spirit upon all flesh…" (Joel 2:28, Acts 2:17).

In the time of the prophet Joel, God's justice was tempered with mercy if men and women would repent. Musicians today have a wonderful opportunity to sound the trumpet and tell this generation that God has promised to pour out his Spirit on those who will repent and do His will. So, Christian musicians should be reminded of the importance of their musicing today. We as Christian musicians may not see how the problems of this generation can be worked out. However, we should remember that it is our responsibility to be "good and faithful" servants by sounding the trumpet of alarm, and it is God's responsibility to meet their spiritual needs.

Prayer for the Day

Thank You, Lord, that You have made it possible that I may, in some small way, "sound the trumpet alarm." Thank You, Father, that Your justice is tempered with mercy for those who will repent of their sins and believe on the Lord Jesus Christ. I am asking You, Lord, to help me to keep sounding the trumpet in Your holy mountain. Please teach me how to warn the people of this generation that Your justice is sure, and Your mercy endures unto all generations. These things I pray. Amen.

October 8

Is Your Music Noisy?

Ezekiel 26:13 — "And I will cause the noise of thy songs to cease; and the sound of thy harps shall be no more heard."

The Lord God pronounced judgment against Tyre because they had wasted Jerusalem. Tyre was also indulgent in its musicing practices. The Lord (*Adonai* 136) who is the sovereign controller of the universe promised Tyre that He would cause the noise of their songs to cease. Like the music praxis of ancient Tyre, some twenty-first century Christian musicians have become indulgent in their ways of religious musicing. One of the main causes of indulgent musicing is that musicians often become enamored with noise and decibels. Twenty-first century Christian musicians need to be careful not to become self-indulgent, self-serving, performance-oriented noise makers. A sense of musical priority is always appropriate when a Christian is attempting to music unto God.

Notice that Ezekiel 26:3 states, "Therefore thus saith the Lord God; Behold, I am against thee, O Tyrus, and will cause many nations to come up against thee, as the sea causeth his waves to come up." The Lord (*Adonai* 136) God (*Jehovah*

3069) was concerned with the sounds (*qowl* 6963) that the musicians were making with their musical instruments.

The sovereign controller of the universe, who is the autonomous, self-existent God, was not pleased because, among other things, they were producing noise-based music. The Hebrew word used here is *hamown* (1995), which means tumultuous sound. So, the Biblical music lesson is very clear. God hears noise-based music, as we know from Ezekiel 26: 13, and He was not pleased with it. Therefore, it is not a farfetched philosophical concept that God will be displeased when we try to music unto Him with noise-based music that does not bring honor to His divine nature.

The music historian Curt Sachs once stated, "How did the ancient Jews sing? Did they actually cry at the top of their voices? Some students have tried to make us believe that such was the case, and they particularly refer to several of the Psalms that allegedly bear witness of praying in fortissimo. But I suspect them of drawing from translations rather than from the original."[2] So, every Christian musician must be careful that the music he or she musics unto God is not noise-based lest it is considered "noise" and be rejected by Him. Great music historians do not believe that the ancient Hebrew nation musiced unto God with noise. Therefore there is no evidence in or out of the Bible to make us believe that we should music unto God with noisy music.

Song for the Day

Come, Christians, Join to Sing by Christian H. Bateman

Thought for the Day

Since the gospel of Jesus Christ is a message of rest, noise-based musicing is an incongruent attempt at accomplishing an atmosphere of stability, confidence, trust and rest.

October 9

Righteous Musicians Sing and Rejoice

Proverbs 29:6— "In the transgression of an evil man there is a snare: but the righteous doth sing and rejoice."

Are you a Christian musician who has a singing heart instead of merely a musician who sings? In other words, are you a rejoicing musician? It is one thing to sing songs about rejoicing, and it is entirely another to rejoice when you music unto God.

When trouble comes, do you proclaim God's power and love, or do you let Satan lead you into depression? God's inspired Word teaches us that the righteous sing and rejoice. It doesn't say that the righteous sing and rejoice only in the good times; it simply states that if you are righteous, you will sing and rejoice. Ouch!

Verse eight of this proverb tells us that the scornful set things on fire, but the righteous "turn away wrath." As a righteous musician, you have the opportunity to use singing as a means of grace that can keep someone from sitting in the seat of the scornful (see Psalm 1). The Bible teaches that there is a difference in an evil person's and a righteous person's actions. An evil person is ensnared by his or her sin, and the righteous person sings and rejoices in the LORD who is willing and able to deliver the Christian out of life's troubles.

If you have been ensnared by some trick of the enemy of your soul, do not give up spiritually. Tell Jesus that you are sorry and really mean it. I Chronicles 16:10 and Psalm 105:3 both say, "Glory ye in his holy name: let the heart of them rejoice that seek the LORD." Rejoice, because only a person who remains evil has to remain ensnared. Remember that in I John 2:1 there is an admonition to us— "My little children, these things write I unto you that ye sin not. And if any man sin, we have an advocate with the Father, Jesus Christ the righteous." Wow! Jesus is right now sitting at the right hand of the Father praying for us. He is praying for us because he cares about us very much. We know this of a surety because Romans 8:34 states, "Who is he that condemneth? It is Christ that died, yea rather, that is risen again, who is even at the right hand of God, who also maketh intercession for us." If Jesus is praying for us, and we know that He is from this Scripture, we can make it through all the troubles of life.

Song for the Day

Our Great Savior by J. Wilbur Chapman

Thought for the Day

Always remember that Jesus gently entreats the Christian, and Satan accuses us and tells us there is no hope.

October 10

Choosing Blessing and Life

Deuteronomy 30:19 — "I call heaven and earth to record this day against you, that I have set before you life and death, blessing and cursing: therefore choose life, that both thou and thy seed may live."

This verse is part of a covenant God made to Moses for the Children of Israel when they were in the land of Moab. The LORD called heaven and earth to record that they had a choice to make between life and death. God's will for them was that they would choose blessing and life. However, since they were free moral agents, the final choice was theirs to make.

As a Christian musician, you once chose to accept life, which comes with the blessings of God as a concomitant to that choice. Along the way, your attitude may have caused you to accept the council of the ungodly, and thereby you may at this point in your life be sitting in the seat of the scornful. If you have chosen to become scornful and bitter in your spirit, you are choosing cursing and ultimately spiritual death for you and your children (see Psalm 1).

If you have chosen to love, forgive, obey and to accept life and blessing, you are on the right spiritual path. Your children can read your silent actions like they would a book. If you are bearing scornful, sour fruit, you are poisoning your soul and the souls of your family. God has promised in this verse of Scripture that He will, and has, set before you the path of life and blessing. I suggest that you take that path today.

Song for the Day

Give Me Jesus by Fanny J. Crosby

Prayer for the Day

Lord, I am asking You to help me to choose life every day that I live. I am also asking You to help me to have and exhibit a forgiving attitude toward others that I work with from day to day. Lord, please help my family to also choose life and blessing over death and cursing. Please help me to bridle my tongue, and at the same time, I am asking You to pour honey over my soul in so much abundance that out of my innermost being will flow rivers of sweet, living water. These things I earnestly pray in Your wonderful name. Amen.

October 11

A Friend Closer than a Brother

Proverbs 18:24 — "A man that hath friends must shew himself friendly: and there is a friend that sticketh closer than a brother."

Today is my brother Nathan's birthday. He is older than me and always fought my battles when I was a child. He is the kind of brother that everyone would like to have. He has always been a dear friend to me.

Since I have such a wonderful friend in my brother, I have an enriched concept of how wonderful a friend Jesus Christ can be to me, or to any Christian for that matter. My brother Nathan has always been there for me throughout my life. However, my Bible teaches me that Christ is a friend that will even stick closer than my brother Nathan.

My brother Nathan is the kind of person that I like to introduce to others. I often brag on him to my other friends and business acquaintances. Although my brother Nathan is worth bragging on every now and then, my Savior Jesus Christ is worth my continual praise. My relationship with my brother also helps me to trust Jesus never to leave me or forsake me. My elder brother Jesus Christ, my Savior and sanctifier, has been a friend that has stayed close to me ever since I came to know Him.

Song for the Day

Friendship with Jesus by Joseph C. Ludgate

Thought for the Day

Everyone should have friends. However, many lonely people do not know what a friend Jesus can be to them. Today, tell someone about your friend and Savior Jesus Christ.

October 12

Chenaniah was Skillful and Faithful

I Chronicles 15:22 — "And Chenaniah, chief of the Levites, was for song: he instructed about the song, because he was skilful."

This verse of Scripture is loaded with pertinent musical and spiritual information. So, let's dig in! Have you ever wondered how this Levite became chief of the Levite musicians? Let us consider that this musician came to prominence because he was a skillful musician. The Hebrew words *yacar* (3256) and *biyn* (995) connote that he was a cunning performer who was knowledgeable enough to be a music instructor to the other Levite musicians.

It is never easy for a minister of music who is very busy to take time to search out the history and meaning of the music he or she leads others in singing or playing in the church service, but it is a part of a musician's faithfulness. Personal practice is very time consuming, and so is giving lessons to other church musicians. Encouraging those who study music with us to practice, digging out spiritual meanings in the music, directing choral and instrumental rehearsals, and working with soloists is exhausting —but very worthwhile. Holding rehearsals when key members are absent is frustrating and challenging.

Faithfulness and a good attitude on the part of the minister of music are essential to an efficacious music ministry. I often think of the words of Jesus in Matthew 25:21 — "His lord said unto him, Well done, thou good and faithful servant: thou hast been faithful over a few things, I will make thee ruler over many things: enter thou into the joy of thy lord."

Song for the Day

Jesus, My Strength, My Hope by Charles Wesley

Prayer for the Day

I want to thank You, Lord, for giving me the opportunity to music to and with other Christian musicians. Please help me to never lose the wonder of musicing with others unto You. As a Christian musician, help me to be a good and faithful musical servant. Lord, help me to be ever aware that if I am not a good servant, all my musicing and all my leading will be in vain. Amen.

October 13

Appointed to Humbly Minister

I Chronicles 16:4— "And he appointed certain of the Levites to minister before the ark of the LORD, and to record, and to thank and praise the LORD God of Israel."

The Hebrew word *nathan* (5414) which has been translated appointed in this verse, is used in the Old Testament with great latitude. In this verse, it connotes to assign or to commit. King David assigned or committed the Levite musicians to minister to Jehovah *Elohim* (3068, 430) the self-existent, eternal God who is the supreme, exceeding God. The word certain does not appear in the original text, so this appointment was not an esoteric calling for a small number of musicians, but rather that God appointed all these musicians to minister unto Him.

The Hebrew word *sharath* (8334) translated minister means to serve, wait on, or minister as a menial worshipper. These Levite musicians were by no means menials. However, they were instructed to minister in the spirit of humility like the most menial worshipper who worshipped Jehovah Elohim.

As kings and priests unto God (see Revelation 1:6) we, as Christian musicians, are appointed by our heavenly Father to minister musically unto God and His people. No matter how accomplished we are as musicians, we are commanded to wait on or serve others with our musicing in the spirit of humility.

Song for the Day

I Then Shall Live by Gloria Gaither

Thought for the Day

The most educated, prepared and qualified Christian

musicians that I have had the privilege to work with were also down-to-earth, humble musicians.

October 14

Appointed to Record, Thank and Praise

I Chronicles 16:4— "And he appointed certain of the Levites to minister before the ark of the LORD, and to record, and to thank and praise the LORD God of Israel."

Yesterday we considered the appointment of the Levite musicians to minister in the spirit of humility. Today we are going to discuss the words record, thank and praise. The Hebrew word *zakar* (2143) which was translated "record" means to remember. Before a congregation of believers can truly worship, they need to remember. Our musicing needs to cause them to remember who God is, what He is like, what He has done, and what He will do for those who love and serve Him.

After we have led the congregation in remembering God's goodness, then we need to lead them in musicing that will cause them to be thankful. A Christian who remembers will become a thankful worshipper. The Hebrew word *yadah* (3034) that has been translated thank means to reach out or to extend the hands. True heartfelt thanksgiving to God will cause the assembly of believers to revere God and to reach out in avowal with extended hands to God.

When the congregation of believers has musiced unto God with recording and thanking, they are then ready to give praise unto God. The word praise put for the Hebrew word *halal* (1984) means to be clear or to boast. Recording and praising will cause Christians who worship to brag and boast about Jehovah Elohim. As they do so, they will be lifted up in the most holy faith.

Song for the Day

I Come With Joy by Brian Wren

Thought for the Day

I Chronicles 16:4 gives us an Old Testament formula for musical worship. It is simple but profound—record, thank and then praise.

October 15

Musicians who Ministered

Ezekiel 40:44— "And without the inner gate were the chambers of the singers in the inner court..."

Bible expositors have had various opinions on this Old Testament text. Many of them simply ignored it as though it was extraneous material without meaning. Others ignored the word *shiyr* (7788) translated "singers," which meant singer-players. Some believe that this Scripture refers to the chambers where the Levite musicians lived.

Matthew Henry believed that

"Some [chambers] were for the singers, v.44. It should seem that they were first provided for before any other that attended [ministered] this temple-service, to intimate, not only that the singing of psalms should still continue a gospel ordinance, but that the gospel should furnish all that embrace it with abundant matter of joy and praise, and give them occasion to *break forth into singing*, which is often foretold concerning gospel times..."[3]

You are probably thinking, "How could this quaint esoteric text from the Bible have meaning to musicians in the twenty-first century?" There are at least two thoughts that are worth considering. First, the Levite musicians' chambers were in very close proximity to the place of worship in the Temple. For some reason, God wanted these musicians to live very close to their place of music ministry. Evidently, Jehovah wanted them to dwell close to where they met with God and experienced His presence during worship. Perhaps Christian musicians may learn from this Old Testament example that we all need to dwell close to where true worship takes place. These musicians lived in the inner court of Jehovah's Temple.

Second, this Scripture is proof that the ancient church took care of the Levite music ministers who regularly musiced unto Jehovah. In this age of financial affluence, the twenty-first century church must take care of its music ministers. (See Numbers18:21, Nehemiah 11:23, 13:5, 13:10.)

The priests and the Levite musicians were described as those (vs. 46) who came "near to the LORD to minister unto him." The Bible example in this passage of Scripture is very clear. One who would wish to minister unto the Lord, both then and now, must live in such a manner that he could and can come near to the LORD to minister unto Him!

Song for the Day

O for a Heart to Praise My God by Charles Wesley

October 16

"Taste of my Supper"

St. Luke 14:16-24— "Then said he unto him, A certain man made a great supper, and bade many: And sent his servant at supper time to say to them that were bidden, Come; for all things are now ready. And they all with one consent began to make excuse… For I say unto you, That none of those men which were bidden shall taste of my supper."

This Bible lesson that Jesus taught has a pleasant beginning but a sad ending. In this parable, it is easy to visualize a great many people who have been called to a feast at God's great table. I have lived long enough to observe many young men and women who were called by God to serve Him. They traveled on the college bus with me for thousands of miles. They feasted at the Lord's table as they musiced unto God. I must admit with sadness that they have not all continued to heed His call, follow His will, and feast at His table.

Galatians 5:7 asks the important question, "Ye did run well; who did hinder you that ye should not obey the truth?" Although God sent His servant to admonish them, while they were in Bible college to use their musical talents for the Lord, someone or something has caused some of them to fail to continue to give their music talents back to God. Nothing in this world is important enough to cause them to stop musicing unto God.

Over the years, when I faced burnout, the only thing that would help was to find a place of prayer and pour out my troubles to the Lord. Jesus always listened patiently and never accused me or made fun of me. After the depression went away, most of the time I would realize that I had been listening to the wrong voice.

When I read this parable taught by Jesus, I am reminded that whatever it takes to keep my appointment at God's supper is worth it. I want to make sure that I keep oil in my spiritual lamp because I have been invited to taste of God's great supper.

Song for the Day

Come and Dine by C.B. Widmeyer

Thought for the Day

When I was in junior high school, I was on the track team. I found out in a hurry that it was much easier to begin a race well than it was to finish successfully. The same is true when it comes to running this Christian race!

Prayer for the Day

Lord, You are the one that controls the universe that You created. Please help me to keep oil in my spiritual lamp so that I will be able to have the strength to keep musicing for You. I am asking You to open my understanding of Your Word so that it may feed my soul. Please give me the unction and anointing of the Holy Spirit for daily service for You. LORD, I know that it isn't by my might or by my own power, but by Your Spirit that I may have an efficacious music ministry. Thank You, LORD, for caring about me and for loving me enough to give Your only Son for my sin. These things I pray with a grateful heart. Amen.

October 17

Singing to Remember

Psalm 30:4 — "Sing unto the LORD, O ye saints of his, and give thanks at the remembrance of his holiness."

Many times in the Book of Psalms we are admonished to "sing unto the LORD." As a matter of fact, the Hebrew title for the Book of Psalms is the *Cepher Tehillim* (5612, 8416) which means the Scroll of Praises. This verse from the Scroll of Praises specifically admonishes those who are "saints of his" to sing unto Jehovah. It is a good thing for the unregenerate person to sing about God, but this psalm is directed to the redeemed. This lyric poem is identified in the superscription as a *mizmowr shiyr* (2167, 7892) which the AV renders a psalm song. These two words mean a song set to instrumental music. So, we justly gather that it is a praise song (poem) set to instrumental music. Furthermore, it is a song of thanks and remembrance.

The poet remembers that the LORD has lifted him up, healed him, brought his soul from the grave, made him stand strong, as well as other wonderful things. Although he has many needs, the self-existent, eternal God, who not only was but is alive, has and will deliver him from his troubles. Christian musicians, being prone to melancholy, fail to have the attitude of this psalmist. Because they get depressed, they "sing the blues" about their troubles rather than remembering that it is "amazing what praising can do" for the Christian who is depressed. Ministering musicians are so intensely involved in their busy little "cloudy world" that they fail to take advantage of the means of grace that will build them up in the "most holy faith." These depressed musicians lead others in worship but fail to partake of the divine fruit that is on God's table.

The psalmist admonishes these musicians to "Sing unto the Lord." He also emphasizes the importance of singing songs of praise that will cause the "saints" to remember Jehovah's holiness (*quodesh* 6944), which means remembering "most holy" things about God.

Why not stop whining right now and start singing God's praises as you call to remembrance all the wonderful things God has done for you. Surely you, as a musician, know an appropriate praise chorus that is fitting for your situation. I suggest that you sing out loud so that you can drown out the whispering of Satan. Remember that you will probably remain depressed if you continue to listen to the wrong voice.

Song for the Day

My Burdens Rolled Away by Minnie Steele

Prayer for the Day

I thank You, Lord! I thank You for bringing to my memory all the times You have come to my deliverance. I thank You for saving and sanctifying power that is real in my life. Please, Lord, accept my songs of Your deliverance which I am singing unto You as a sacrifice of praise. I am asking that, as I take the journey from the natural to the supernatural to give You praises from deep within my heart, that my prayer will ascend to heaven where You dwell in power and splendor. Amen.

October 18

What if Your Musician Son was Chosen Last?

I Chronicles 25: 8-9 — "And they cast lots, ward against ward, as well the small as the great, the teacher as the scholar. Now the first lot came forth for Asaph to Joseph..."

I Chronicles 25: 31 — "The four and twentieth to Romamtiezer, he, his sons, and his brethren, were twelve."

David and his captains separated the sons of Asaph, Heman (Ethan) and Jeduthun to prophesy with singing and with instruments. I can picture this great event in the life of the Levites who were music ministers in the Temple. The Biblical record states, "Now the first lot came forth for Asaph to Joseph..." (verse 9). Wow, think of it, Asaph's son Joseph was chosen first. Think of how fast his father Asaph's heart must have been beating when the first lot fell to Joseph. Asaph had to have been justifiably proud that Jehovah had chosen his son first by the casting of lots.

So, I wish that I could have been there as the choices were being made. Number two went to Jeduthun's son Gadaliah; the third to Zaccur, who was also Asaph's son. The fourth lot fell to Jeduthun's son Izri (who was also called Zeri) and so on down the line, the sons of the chief musicians were chosen one by one by the casting of lots. I cannot help wonder what was going on in Heman's mind as the casting of lots drew near to the end of the Levite sons. When lot 23 fell to Mahazioth, Heman knew that his precious and faithful son Romamtiezer was destined to be last.

No matter how dedicated you are as a Christian musician, it hurts like fire when your child is chosen last. It hurts much worse for one of your children to be chosen last than if it was yourself. Let me remind you that the Biblical record did not put any premium on Joseph being chosen first or any stigma placed on Romamtiezer being chosen last. Romamtiezer's name is just as much on the list of these famous Levite musicians as any of the others. He was listed with the faithful and was given just as much of an opportunity to serve Jehovah with his musicing as any of the other musicians. It would be well to remember that Jesus said in Matthew 19:30, "But many that are first shall be last; and the last shall be first."

The Bible lesson here in First Chronicles is clear. We have no record that Heman or his son were in any way disappointed or upset about position. Wouldn't it be wonderful if we could say that of twenty-first century Christians in regards to their children? It is the explicit stratagem of Satan to get parents upset over which chair is given to their child or who gets the solo in the Christmas production. The thing that should matter to Christian parents is the fact that their children are giving their talents back to the God who gave them musical gifts and graces.

Thought for the Day

There is no Scripture in the Old Testament where it is recorded that the Levite musicians fought over position or place for themselves or their children.

Scripture for the Day

"But many that are first shall be last; and the last shall be first" (Matthew 19:30).

October 19

Postmoderns may Consider You Dated, Dazed and Dumb

Romans 1:16 — "For I am not ashamed of the gospel of Christ: for it is the power of God unto salvation to every one that believeth; to the Jew first, and also to the Greek."

If you are a Christian musician who still ministers with traditional hymns, gospel choruses, and gospel songs you may be discouraged since many postmoderns consider you dated, dazed and just plain dumb. St. Paul declared in this verse that he was not ashamed of the gospel of Christ. If you desire to include more than a long string of praise choruses in your music ministry, so that you can music the whole gospel of Christ, you should not be intimidated or tuck your head as though you were some outdated dunderhead.

This is not to say that there is anything wrong with a string of praise choruses. However, the inspired Word of God declares very clearly that the gospel is the power of God unto salvation. Although praise is essential to Christian worship, it is not expository enough to fulfill all the elements necessary in complete Trinitarian worship.

It is your responsibility to present the whole gospel of Christ who suffered, died and paid the penalty for our sins. It is the responsibility of the Holy Spirit to convict and convince seekers of their need of repentance and forgiveness of sins "unto salvation." It is not the power of your charisma or performance ability, but rather the power of the whole gospel and the power of the Holy Spirit, that is the power of God.

For your musicing unto God to be completely efficacious, it must contain the whole gospel. This is the reason that a thinking minister of music includes gospel songs, gospel hymns, and gospel choruses along with praise music in his or her balanced musical diet for the assembly of believers and seekers who attend worship services. The saint needs to be reminded of what God the Father, God the Son, and God the Holy Spirit have accomplished in the plan of redemption, and the seeker must be made aware of the same things. How can seekers have Godly sorrow that works toward repentance if they do not know what God has done for those who have given their heart to the Lord and have accepted God's forgiveness?

Let me make it very clear, that there is absolutely nothing wrong with a praise chorus sequence in worship. That statement must be qualified with the understanding that a praise sequence should not exceed the attention span of the modern audience. Also, the notion that this sequence must drone on until the minister gets his or her desired overt emotional response from the audience is misguided philosophically. It is important that a congregation of believers sing of the love of God and also testify of their love of God the Father, Son and Holy Spirit.

So, if your musicing presents a clear gospel message, and if your musicing includes traditional gospel music and hymns, take heart: you are on solid philosophical ground. Do it in the right spirit, but square your shoulders and keep presenting the old, old story. When you music, never be ashamed to confront saints and seekers with the claims of the gospel.

Scripture for the Day

"For do I now persuade men, or God? Or do I seek to please men? For if I yet pleased men, I should not be the servant of Christ" (Galatians 1:10).

Chorus for the Day

I Will Serve Thee by William and Gloria Gaither

October 20

Are You a Lively Stone?

I Peter 2:5— "Ye also, as lively stones, are built up a spiritual house, an holy priesthood, to offer up spiritual sacrifices, acceptable to God by Jesus Christ."

Christ, the chief cornerstone, has chosen us and has made us living stones. Once we were dead in trespasses and sins, but now we are living stones. We know from verse nine that we are a chosen generation and a spiritual house.

In the Old Testament, in Malachi 3:3, it is recorded that God purified the sons of Levi so that they might be able to offer unto God an offering in righteousness. The Hebrew word *tsadaqah* (6666) which was translated righteousness in the AV, means sacrificial offerings that were of moral virtue.

A musician that is dead in trespasses and sins is not able to offer musical offerings that are spiritually efficacious. The reason is that righteous "doing" requires righteous "being." To be a part of God's holy priesthood a musician must be a lively stone in Christ Jesus. The word lively which was put for the Greek word *zao* (2198) connotes life, hence to be alive in Christ our Lord.

Why must we offer up spiritual musical sacrifices as we music unto God? The answer is simple. As musical ministers, our musicing may be musical but they will never be acceptable unto God by Christ Jesus unless our offerings are spiritual sacrifices. So, two lessons are taught in I Peter 2:5. First, the musician must be a spiritual person, and his or her musical offerings must be acceptable unto God by Christ Jesus.

Scripture for the Day

"And he shall sit as a refiner and purifier of silver: and he shall purify the sons of Levi, and purge them as gold and silver, that they may offer unto the Lord an offering in righteousness" (Malachi 3:3).

Prayer for the Day

I thank You, Lord, for taking a lifeless, dead rock and transforming me into a lively, living stone. Lord, I am asking You to help me to continue to be a "lively stone." Please continue to build me up so that I will continue to be a useful part of Your spiritual house and a useful ministering servant. I ask You to daily fill me with Your Spirit so that I may offer spiritual musical sacrifices unto You. Please endue me with Your power in order that my musicing will be efficacious. These things I pray in Your strong name. Amen.

October 21

Prayer Makes a Difference

Acts 12:5— "Peter therefore was kept in prison: but prayer was made without ceasing of the church unto God for him."

This Bible lesson recounts Peter's imprisonment, his marvelous release, and how astonished the church was that God had answered their prayer. We may chuckle when we read about a church that prayed and was shocked when Peter showed up at the gate, but we too often react much like them when God answers our prayers.

I remember when the Music Division staff of the college where I worked prayed for a long time for a seven-foot grand piano that was needed for a piano teacher's studio. The staff prayed and I tried to raise money to purchase it, but nothing happened. Then, much to our surprise, a local television station called the college and asked if we would like to have a seven-foot Baldwin that they had recently rebuilt. We were all shocked as we stood around this beautiful instrument that had just been given to the college. We were close to believing that God was not going to supply our needs when we were on the brink of a miracle.

Scripture for the Day

"Confess your faults one to another, and pray one for another, that ye may be healed. The effectual fervent prayer of a righteous man availeth much" (James 5:16).

Thought for the Day

It is one thing to believe that God can supply our needs, but it is another to believe that He will do it.

October 22

The Lord will Rejoice Over You

Deuteronomy 30:8-9 — "And thou shalt return and obey the voice of the LORD, and do all his commandments which I command thee this day. And the LORD thy God will make thee plenteous in every work of thine hand, in the fruit of thy body, and in the fruit of thy cattle, and in the fruit of thy land, for good: for the LORD will again rejoice over thee for good, as he rejoiced over thy fathers."

Israel had disobeyed the law of God and Jehovah had been angry with them. However, this Scripture lesson promises mercy to the penitent and blessing on those who would obey the commandments of Jehovah.

Verse nine explains the thoroughness of how the self-existent, eternal, sovereign God will bless those who keep His commandments. Some ministers of music might say, "I am single, I don't have any cows, and I don't own any land, so how is God going to rejoice over me with prosperity?" God has promised to prosper the obedient by rejoicing over them "for good." Our heavenly Father has promised, on the authority of His Holy Word, that if ministers of music will obey what He tells them to do, that He intends to "do you good," as we know from Deuteronomy 28:63, "… that as the Lord rejoiced over you to do you good, and to multiply you;" and from Jeremiah 32:41, " Yea, I will rejoice over them to do them good, and I will plant them in this land assuredly with my whole heart and with my whole soul."

Hebrews 11:6 tells us, "But without faith it is impossible to please him: for he that cometh to God must believe that he is, and that he is the rewarder of them that diligently seek him." God will prosper those who have faith in Him in every way that matters if they will believe that "He is" and that He actually will keep His Word and reward those who diligently seek Him.

When a Christian musician comes to an understanding of what God is willing and able to do, this wonderful knowledge should bring a smile out of at least one side of his or her mouth! The Christian musician should remember that, on the eternal authority of God's inspired, infallible Word, one cannot fail while God is smiling on his or her music ministry.

Chorus for the Day

I Will Call Upon the Lord by Michael O'Shields

Thought for the Day

It is only natural that a Christian would want people to rejoice while he or she musics unto God. However, it is much more important for God to rejoice over us than our listening audience.

October 23

Heirs of the Kingdom

James 2:5— "Hearken, my beloved brethren, Hath not God chosen the poor of this world rich in faith, and heirs of the kingdom which he hath promised to them that love him?"

This verse is a wonderful thought and a precious promise to them that love the Lord. God has chosen the poor, so that certainly includes me! Though many musicians are "on the short end of the stick" when it comes to this world's goods, they are actually rich. They are rich in the things that really matter. This verse reminds all who read it that those who love the Lord are rich in faith. They are rich because they were adopted into the family of God when He forgave them and redeemed them by His precious blood which was shed on Calvary's cross.

The Christian musician should also remember that God has protected, rewarded, blessed, and called them into His service. Since all those who love the Lord are His sons and daughters, they are rich, because they are God's heirs and will receive a great inheritance that is so great that it is more than we can ask or think.

Christian musician, it is time for you to cheer up! There is no reason for you to let the Devil depress you or to cause you to think negative thoughts. If you truly love the Lord, you are rich in faith now, and God has promised you an inheritance among those who are sanctified. Acts 20:32 tells us, "And now, brethren, I commend you to God, and to the word of his grace, which is able to build you up, and to give you an inheritance among all them which are sanctified." Praise God! What more could you want? You are now rich in grace in this life, and you have an inheritance among the sanctified.

Thought for the Day

Christian musicians do not have anything to whine about. They are rich in grace now and have a rich inheritance in heaven for eternity!

October 24

It is Christ, Not Music, Who Draws Men

St. John 12:32-33 — "And I, if I be lifted up from the earth, will draw all men unto me. This he said, signifying what death he should die."

Christ left no doubt in our minds, in this Bible lesson, that He would die on the cross so that we could be drawn to Him and have forgiveness of sins. He explained in John 12:47, "...I came not to judge the world, but to save the world." So, we know with surety that all who will receive Christ may be saved. Twenty-first-century church musicians must remember that it is our responsibility to sing and play the gospel message, and it is His responsibility to draw all men unto Himself.

There is a great need in this century for men and women to hear expository preaching. There is also a need for expository music ministry so that all will know the message of Christ's suffering, death and resurrection, as well as God's law and His love for all people.

Praise music is wonderful because the blessed Trinity is worthy of all of our praise and adoration. Although our praises are comely for the upright, they are not the complete gospel message. The gospel message is the old, old story of the Christ who left the portals of the Glory World, took on the form of man, and suffered, died on the old rugged cross, paid the full penalty for sin, and was resurrected so that we might have forgiveness of all our sins. It is through Christ and Christ alone that we may be justified through the grace that is extended unto us all. Unless our musicing expounds the full gospel message, it is by far an incomplete ministry.

Are you musicing the full gospel message? Does your musicing tell lost men and women that Christ unselfishly shed His blood for their sins? Do you music regularly that all have sinned and have come short of the glory of God? Does your musicing explain that sin separates mankind from a holy God? Do you sing the entire truth that the wages of sin is eternal death, but the gift of God is eternal life only through our Lord Jesus Christ? Are you are musicing these eternal truths?

Song for the Day

Jesus Calls Us by Cecil F. Alexander

Thought for the Day

As a Christian musician, I want the audience to enjoy my music ministry. However, if that means that I cannot tell them the complete truth, then I must please God rather than my audience.

October 25

Musical Ability Comes from God

I Peter 4:11— "If any man speak, let him speak as the oracles of God; if any man minister, let him do it as of the ability which God giveth: that God in all things may be glorified through Jesus Christ, to whom be praise and dominion for ever and ever. Amen."

As we well know, all musical ability comes from God the creator and owner of music. So, the Christian musician who considers himself or herself a self-made musician is a religious humanist. The Bible says, "If any man minister, let him do it as of the ability which God giveth."

Contrary to popular thought among postmodern, religious humanists, no church musician, performer, music educator or dog catcher who musics unto God does so of his or her own ability. If you are reveling in the fact that you studied trumpet at a prestigious university, you have forgotten that your lips were formed in your mother's womb by the very God who created you and owns music and musical ability. He foreknew that you were going to play the trumpet. So, he formed your lips and your dental structure to make it possible for you to play trumpet well.

This Bible lesson tells all Christian musicians that if they forget where they received their musical talents, their ability to music efficaciously will be hindered by the fact that God will not receive the glory for their musicing.

Prayer for the Day

I thank You, Lord, for preparing Your servant, even before I was born, to be a ministering musician. Lord, I give all my musical gifts back to You. I give all my musical worship to You. I also give You the glory for all of the musical accomplishments of my life. Help me always to remember that You will not share Your glory with any Christian musician. These things I bring to You. Amen.

Thought for the Day

If God created everything, and He most certainly did, He created talent. Therefore, all talent belongs to Him. So, we do not have rights over talent; we only have responsibilities and opportunities to use our God-given gifts for Him.

October 26

Christian Musicians are Called from Darkness to Light

I Peter 2:9 — "But ye are a chosen generation, a royal priesthood, an holy nation, a peculiar people; that ye should shew forth the praises of him who hath called you out of darkness into his marvellous light."

Today we are going to consider five thoughts found in I Peter 2:9. First, we are a chosen generation; second, a royal priesthood; third, a holy nation; fourth, a peculiar people; fifth, a people called from the darkness of sin unto the marvelous light of salvation.

It is a marvel to me that I have been called or chosen by God to music unto Him. I often wonder why God has chosen me to be a part of His royal priesthood. Why me? I am small. I do not have perfect pitch or even excellent relative pitch. I am not from an ecclesiastical background. I was raised on an eighty-acre farm in eastern Kansas. I was a chief nobody among those who were considered to be nobody. But praise God, He lifted me out of the deep, miry clay of sin and set my feet upon the rock Christ Jesus. He has called me to show forth His praises by musicing about His matchless and wonderful name.

God has also made it possible for me, a Kansas farmer, to be a part of His holy nation. He has also purified my heart by His great power. Thank God that my Savior Jesus Christ suffered to sanctify me as one of His people (see Hebrews 13:12).

God has made me a part of His peculiar people. The Greek word *peripoiesis* (4047) which was translated as "peculiar" means a purchased people. I am peculiarly purchased in that Christ did not purchase me with money, but through His own blood that He shed for my sins on the cross at Calvary. I was such an awful sinner that my changed life shows forth the praises of God's wonderful name. He has called me from the awful darkness of my sinful life, into the wonderful light of his presence.

Song for the Day

The Light of the World is Jesus by Philip P. Bliss

Thought for the Day

It is no wonder that Christian musicians are constantly praising God with music. They have been called from awful, sinful darkness into the marvelous light of God's presence.

October 27

God will Guide His Musicians

Psalm 27:6— "And now shall mine head be lifted up above mine enemies round about me: therefore will I offer in his tabernacle sacrifices of joy; I will sing, yea, I will sing praises unto the LORD."

In verse five of this psalm, David declared that "in the time of trouble he shall hide me in his pavilion" (*sok* 5520). This Hebrew word connotes a covert den entwined with boughs. David had faith that God would hide him securely away in a den that God had prepared with entwined branches so thickly woven that David's enemies could not find him. David was speaking figuratively of God's ability to protect him. It is no wonder that the psalmist David declared that he would go to church and shout for joy as he sang praises to God. Surely every musician should shout for joy when he or she remembers the many times that God has given divine protection.

It would be a good thing if you would drop on your knees right now and give God a sacrifice of praise and joy. It would strengthen you spiritually if you told the Lord how much you appreciate Him for hiding you from your enemy, Satan. Thank your heavenly Father for protecting you from Satan who has been going about as a roaring lion seeking for you, as a Christian musician, to destroy you spiritually. Satan hates Christian musicians because they not only praise God with music, but they also lead whole congregations in praising and worshipping God. So, he tries, in every subtle way that he can think of, to destroy them. However, they have a special *"sok"* in which they can hide from the wiles of the devil.

Song for the Day

He Leadeth Me by Joseph H. Gilmore

Prayer for the Day

I thank You, Lord, for being my protector. Thank You for hiding me in this little pavilion so well woven with Your protecting branches that Satan cannot find me or get in to devour my soul. Lord, I am no match for Satan. So, I am going to stay in this little protective place as long as Satan is running around trying to destroy my soul and my music ministry. When I am troubled and afraid, help me to trust in You. Help me to turn to You ,the "lifter up of my head," for protection from the enemy of my soul. Praise God! You are worthy of praise. Thank You in advance for Your complete protection throughout this entire day. Amen.

October 28

The Lord is the Musician's Shield

Psalm 28:7 — "The Lord is my strength and my shield; my heart trusted in him, and I am helped: therefore my heart greatly rejoiceth; and with my song will I praise him."

The psalmist declared that he was helped (*azar* 5826) or surrounded by the protection of Jehovah, the self-existent, eternal God who is alive. In the time of trouble, the musician David was able to receive strength from God. David was surrounded by the protection of Jehovah. The Hebrew word *magen* (4043) which was rendered shield in the AV means a protector, and it sometimes referred to the rough, tough, scaly hide of the crocodile. The musician David could trust because God had placed a tough protection all the way around him. David's enemies could not destroy him because of this thorough protection.

Christian musician, you need to remember that you are surrounded by God's strength and shield. God will not allow you to be overcome spiritually and mentally if you stay inside the crocodile's hide He has provided for you. If the battle is too tough for you, crawl inside of this tough protection and the enemy of your soul, Satan, will not be able to get to you!

Song for the Day

God Will Take Care of You by Civilla D. Martin

Thought for the Day

Musicians who are self-starters often try to solve their own problems rather than fleeing to God and the means of grace that He has provided for them.

October 29

Finding God's Will

Matthew 4:19— "And he saith unto them, Follow me, and I will make you fishers of men."

When Jesus was walking on the shore of the Sea of Galilee, He saw Peter and Andrew net fishing out of a boat. Jesus, knowing that they were fishermen by trade, appealed to them in the language of a fisherman. Jesus did not call them to build boats. He called them to "fish" because that is what they did well. He called them to take the old "gospel net" and use it to catch men and women for the Lord. God calls men and women who have musical talent to minister for Him with music. Christian musician, God has called you to do what He has given you the gifts and graces to accomplish successfully for His kingdom.

Many talented Christian musicians mistake their call to music ministry with some other calling that seems to be, at the time, more exotic or noble. Christian musicians must remember that there is nothing more noble than finding and doing the will of God. There is no profession that is more valuable or noble than using your God-given musical gifts in Christ's kingdom.

Song for the Day

Holy Spirit Be My Guide by Mildred Cope

Prayer for the Day

I thank You, Lord, for giving me the gifts and graces to music unto You. Lord, I am asking You to strengthen me and mold me into being a better musical servant in Your kingdom. I am willing to be Your musical servant. Show me how to be a musical fisher of men. Please do not let me consume my musical talents on my own lusts and pleasures. Help me to give my all to Your kingdom. These things I pray in Your wonderful name. Amen.

October 30

Daniel Purposed in His Heart

Daniel 1:8 — "But Daniel purposed in his heart that he would not defile himself..."

When Daniel was taken captive and was placed in the court

of King Nebuchadnezzar, he purposed in his heart not to defile himself with the king's meat and drink. Little did he know that he would soon have to make a choice not to defile himself with the *qeren, mashrokiy, kithara, sebbeka, pescanterin*, and *sumphonia* which were used with various kinds of Babylonian, false worship music. These instruments which accompanied the music were played as a concomitant to the worship of the king of Babylon. The significance of the music is not fully explained in Daniel 3:5, 7, 10 and 15. Although their musical usage was not thoroughly explained in the account in the Book of Daniel, we know that it was not the mere use of these instruments that Daniel resisted. It was the significance of what this musical worship represented that Daniel resisted.

Christian musicians need to be careful that they do not get so caught up in music-making that they fail to consider what the music represents by association. It isn't only what music styles a Christian uses, but also how he or she uses the music that makes a difference.

Thought for the Day

The older I get the more convinced I am that it does not make much sense to start following Jesus without first making a decision to keep following Him throughout one's lifetime.

Prayer for the Day

Lord, I thank You for the Holy Spirit that gives me guidance in musicing unto the blessed Trinity. Please help me to purpose in my heart not to defile myself with the world's music that does not honor You. Please never let me be squeezed into the world's mold of musicing unto man and musicing for man's glory. I am asking You, Lord, to help me never to worship man or music. Help me to not bow down to the art of music, but to only use worship music that will bring honor to the one true God. These things I pray in Your name. Amen.

October 31

A Musician's Awareness of God's Faithfulness

Psalm 37:25 — "I have been young, and now am old; yet have I not seen the righteous forsaken, nor his seed begging bread."

The musician David had seen a lot of life by the time that he penned this psalm. He had seen good times and bad times. However, he assessed that God takes care of the righteous. As a musician, you may feel forsaken at times, but you must remember that David was correct in believing that God will not forget His children. Satan will try to influence your thinking to try to get you to believe that God may not take care of you.

First, you must remember that as Hebrews 13:5 states, "...I will never leave thee, nor forsake thee." Second, you must remember that as the musician David looked back over his life, he could testify that he had never seen God's seed "begging bread." In tough times, you need to remember that God takes care of the righteous financially.

Hebrews 13:5 admonishes you as a Christian to "Let your conversation be without covetousness; and be content with such things as ye have..." There is a difference between having real needs and merely wanting things. Although God has promised to take care of the righteous, there are a few requirements for Christians. These are: be righteous, be content, and don't be covetous. If all of us will follow these simple guidelines, we have God's Word of promise that our heavenly Father will see us through good times and bad times.

Song for the Day

Great is Thy Faithfulness by Thomas O. Chisholm

Thought for the Day

Someone has said, "Money may not be what is first in

many Christian musician's lives, but it is way ahead of whatever is second in their lives!"

Endnotes:

1. A.Z. Idelsohn, *Jewish Music: In Its Historical Development* (New York: Tudor, 1948) 35-36.

2. Curt Sachs, *The Rise of Music in the Ancient World, East and West* (New York: Norton, 1978) 80.

3. Matthew Henry, *Joshua-Esther.* vol. IV in *Matthew Henry's Commentary* (McLean, VA: MacDonald Publishing Company, *n.d.*) 985.

NOVEMBER

November 1

Lead or Be Led

Psalm 59:2-3 — "Deliver me from the workers of iniquity, and save me from bloody men. For, lo, they lie in wait for my soul: the mighty are gathered against me; not for my transgression, nor for my sin, O Lord."

Although we do not like to dwell on anything negative, the world is not, and has never been, a friend of grace. Every Christian musician must be aware that he or she will either be a leader or will by default become the victim of some other leadership.

My wife and I were walking the other day at the mall and a lady started walking with us. After some small talk, my wife immediately began to thank the Lord for His goodness to us. The lady said that she had been raised a Baptist, but she was now a "pagan." I think she was without doubt mixed up on her terminology, but I was impressed that my wife did not let her dominate the conversation when it came to spiritual matters.

A Christian has the choice to let non-Christians control the conversation or to lead by proclaiming the name of Jesus, even when it is not popular to take a stand. If a Christian continually keeps silent when the name of God is reviled or made light of, that Christian's faith becomes damaged. So, stand up for Jesus, and Satan will have to withdraw, and Jesus your advocate will stand up for you!

Song for the Day

Stand Up, Stand Up for Jesus by George Duffield

Prayer for the Day

Heavenly Father, I want to thank You for helping me

not to be intimidated by those who do not love and serve You. Thank You for giving me the strength to stand up for Your righteous and holy name. I am asking You to keep delivering me from the subtle influences of those who are "workers of iniquity." Thank You for delivering me from those who "lie in wait for my soul." Help me to praise Your name and to resist the false philosophies of this present world. These things I am praying in Your strong name. Amen.

November 2

Spirit-Filled Music is Edifying

Isaiah 29:13 — "Wherefore the Lord said, Forasmuch as this people draw near me with their mouth, and with their lips do honour me, but have removed their heart far from me, and their fear toward me is taught by the precept of men."

Henry Halley, speaking of Ephesians 5:18-21 states, "Hymn singing is by far the most natural, simplest, best loved and by all odds the most spiritually stimulating of all the exercises of religious meetings."[1] Why is the music ministry of a Spirit-filled musician edifying to the congregation? One thing is sure, Spirit-filled musicing doesn't start with a score or with an instrument, but rather with a Spirit-filled musician. This music begins as a result of heart-felt, religious knowledge and concurrent emotions. Since there is the knowledge of sins forgiven and the marvelous keeping power of God, this awareness brings about spiritual emotions in the process of music-making.

There is more to religious music-making than knowledge and emotion, but there is no evidence in the Old or New Testament that would prohibit or exclude emotion and meaning from religious music. Spirit-filled music making should express strong, generalized feelings caused by a series of complex, spiritual reactions brought about as a result of a holy heart-life.

The musician who performs sacred music in or out of church has an obligation to be true to the message of the music he or she is performing. As I have often stated, it is one thing to sing about God, but it is entirely another to know the God that you are musicing about. Mark 7:6 records the words of Jesus, who quoted Isaiah 29:13 to the Pharisees when speaking to them about vain worship. "He answered and said unto them, Well hath Esaias prophesied of you hypocrites, as it is written, This people honoureth me with their lips, but their heart is far from me." Sacred musicing is nothing more than human performance and is not an act of true worship unless the musician is living in unbroken fellowship with God.

Song for the Day

Guard Your Heart by Steve Green

November 3

Christian Musicians Must Reason

Isaiah 1:1 — "Come now, and let us reason together, saith the LORD…"

I Samuel 12:7 — "Now therefore stand still, that I may reason with you…"

Romans 12:1 — "I beseech you therefore, brethren, by the mercies of God, that ye present your bodies a living sacrifice, holy, acceptable unto God, which is your reasonable service."

Acts 17:2 — "And Paul, as his manner was, went in unto them, and three sabbath days reasoned with them…"

Isaiah, in his prophecy to Judah, uses the Hebrew word *yakach* (3198) which has been translated reason in the AV. It means "to cause one to decide to be right." In Samuel's exhortation to Israel, the Hebrew word *shaphat* (8199) was used, and it has been rendered reason in the AV. It means literally to "pronounce sentence or to execute a judgment" on someone. The Romans writer used the Greek word *logikos* (3050), which the AV translated as reasonable. This Greek word means to use rational thinking or the use of logic. St. Paul used the Greek word *dialegomai* (1256) in his three-day disputation in the synagogue at Thessalonica. It is translated reason in the AV and means to dispute or argue thoroughly with logic.

God's Word and God's way are always logical and reasonable. If Satan is trying to get you to think unreasonable thoughts or follow a path in life that is unreasonable, resist him in the name of Jesus Christ, and he will have to flee from you. He will not have to flee because of your logic or what you believe, but rather because you invoke the strong name and power of the Lord Jesus Christ, who is sitting at the right hand of the Father making intercession for you at this very moment.

God is never the author of confusion or irrational reasoning. Musicians are emotional and sometimes irrational thinkers. Sometimes they just do not think before they leap. If your thinking right now does not line up to the Word of God, change your thinking. If you cannot defend your thinking with God's reasonable Word, then what you are thinking is wrong. Do not leap if you haven't prayed and followed the clear leading of the Holy Spirit. If you are in doubt, don't do it!

If a thorough discussion of God's Word proves your reasoning to be faulty, you are, as my father used to say, "leading your ducks into a poor pond." Don't speak or act before you think. Be sure that you never act in haste. Satan whispers, "You must act fast." Our wise heavenly Father says, "Come now, let us reason together."

Thought for the Day

You can always discern who is speaking to you by how quickly the mysterious voice wants you to act. Satan's voice is subtle but urgent—God's voice is gentle, is never in a hurry, and always gives you time to pray and read God's word.

November 4

Musicing (Part 1)—To God and People

Ephesians 5:19-20— "Speaking to yourselves in psalms and hymns and spiritual songs, singing and making melody in your heart to the Lord; Giving thanks always for all things unto God and the Father in the name of our Lord Jesus Christ."

Although worship music should be to "one another" and "to yourselves," it should always function as a musical offering to God and not a musical entertainment for the people. Since worship music should cause the people to "muse" or think it should never be an amusement. It should edify (draw the people closer to God) rather than to entertain the congregation. So, the fact that church music is not the primary communicator of grace does not mean that it is not very important or that it does not matter. On the contrary, church music matters very much when it comes to the matter of communicating grace.

Scripture Thought for the Day

1 Corinthians 1:18— "For the preaching of the cross is to them that perish foolishness; but unto us which are saved it is the power of God."

November 5

Musicing (Part 2)— Spiritual Things

1 Corinthians 2:13 — "Which things also we speak, not in the words which man's wisdom teacheth, but which the Holy Ghost teacheth; comparing spiritual things with spiritual."

Music often takes preeminence over preaching in many post-modern and post-postmodern churches. When it does, that assembly of believers is following a philosophy based on the wisdom of the matrix of this present world rather than the wisdom which the Holy Spirit teaches. Postmodern and post- postmodern church philosophy considers a longer sermon and a shorter period of singing to be "weak" and therefore unwise. I Corinthians 1:25 reminds us that "...the foolishness of God is wiser than men; and the weakness of God is stronger than men."

Corporate worship through singing is a valuable means of grace to the believer. Singing can be a valuable teaching tool. Singing can be used by the Holy Spirit to convict and convert sinners. However, I Corinthians 1:18 states that preaching is "the power of God." Music, although it has power, is never spoken of in the Bible as the "power of God." Verse twenty of chapter one of I Corinthians says, "Where is the wise? where is the scribe? where is the disputer of this world? hath not God made foolish the wisdom of this world?"

Scripture Thought for the Day

1 Corinthians 1:19 — "For it is written, I will destroy the wisdom of the wise, and will bring to nothing the understanding of the prudent."

November 6

Musicing (Part 3)—Christ Crucified

1 Corinthians 1:18 — "For the preaching of the cross is to them that perish foolishness; but unto us which are saved it is the power of God."

The Sophists were ancient Greek philosophers notorious for their specious arguments. Their arguments sounded logical and good but often were far from being correct. The disputers were philosophic debaters involved in controversial discussions. Paul declared here that God has shown how insipid their arguments were. The arguments of the Sophists were, as verse twenty tells us, based on the wisdom of the *aion* (165) or the present system of the age. It was wisdom based on the matrix of Satan.

What does the Scripture lesson in 1 Corinthians 1:18 mean to the twenty-first century church? First of all, there is and always has been a war going on between the wisdom of God and the specious arguments of the present age. Every Christian musician should be sure that he or she is following Biblical wisdom when developing a music ministry philosophy. Second, there are very logical-sounding arguments that are prevalent today that simply do not line up with Scripture. Beware that you are not led astray by what seems to make sense, at least by the world's standards. If your philosophy has caused you not to keep the main thing the main thing, then it is faulty.

Scripture Thought for the Day

1 Corinthians 1:20 — "Where is the wise? where is the scribe? where is the disputer of this world? hath not God made foolish the wisdom of this world?"

November 7

Musicing (Part 4)—Is it Foolishness?

1 Corinthians 2:14— "But the natural man receiveth not the things of the Spirit of God: for they are foolishness unto him: neither can he know them, because they are spiritually discerned."

Ancient philosophers believed that music could have a profound moral effect on the hearer. "All ancient peoples of whom we have knowledge gave music a place of honor, they considered it a potent religious and moral force, intimately related to the most formal, as well as the most informal aspects of life."[2] It has only been the product of modern man's mind that music is amoral. Although philosophers and musicians have argued for centuries about how music affects us or exactly what moral effect music had on the auditor and the performer, they have always believed that music had a message.

Philosophers have also always believed that music had great power over everyone. It has only been since the twentieth century that some Christian philosophers have concluded that style in music is neutral and therefore amoral. Under this new "liberated" philosophy, anything goes in church music. To them, church music exists in an absurd universe and is a standardless art. Since church music is without absolutes or any standard of correctness, it is merely a matter of personal taste. These modern church music philosophers quote St. Matthew 7:1, "Judge not, that ye be not judged." They purport that Jesus put an end to judgment when it comes to Christian living.

Thought for the Day

You will change the world around you with the music you perform. Will it be a better world?

November 8

Musicing (Part 5)—The Gospel

Romans 1:16 — "For I am not ashamed of the gospel of Christ: for it is the power of God unto salvation to every one that believeth; to the Jew first, and also to the Greek."

I am not sure that St. Paul was a musician; at least he never mentioned that he personally musiced unto God. However, he mentioned musicing unto God in his epistles. As a matter of fact, what he had to say about music and musicing unto God was very pungent. He may or may not have musiced unto God but one thing I believe: if he did, I am sure that his musicing was "gospel" musicing and was done without fear or favor, because he definitely was not ashamed of the gospel of Christ.

Paul showed during his life and ministry that, as he said in his epistle to the church at Rome, he was "not ashamed of the gospel of Christ." I wish that all Christian musicians understood that sacred musicing is not primarily about music as an art form, but rather about musicing the gospel of Jesus Christ that makes it the power of God. The Bible never says that music is itself the power of God.

David, who was a psalmist and a great Old Testament musician, said in Psalm 40:9, "I have preached righteousness in the great congregation: lo, I have not refrained my lips, O Lord, thou knowest." David understood, even in the Old Testament dispensation long before Christ came to earth, that he needed to music righteousness to the congregation. So, it is not about a Christian musician's musical ability or performance skills, but rather about musicing the gospel of our Lord and Savior Jesus Christ, that makes a Christian's musicing efficacious.

Thought for the Day

Sacred musicing should always be from a ministry and a referential standpoint. The music part of music is vitally important, but the gospel of Jesus Christ is brought to the experience of musicing from outside of the formal properties of the music.

November 9

I Will Declare Your Name

Hebrews 2:12 — "...I will declare thy name unto my brethren, in the midst of the church will I sing praise unto thee."

The Scripture in Paul's letter to the Hebrews is a bit difficult to understand. Clarke, Whedon, and Barnes all agree that this direct quote of Psalm 22:22 is messianic and therefore referring to Christ in the Hebrew letter. If this is a correct exegesis, then Christ is not ashamed to call us brethren. With this in mind, we can deduce that Christ is approving and participating in singing God's praises in public worship. No wonder the child of God claims Jesus as our elder brother. What an encouragement it is to the Christian musician to realize that Jesus, who sits at the right hand of the Father, is not ashamed to call us "brethren."

Next is the statement that in the midst of the church, Jesus will sing God's praises. I must admit that again, this statement is very difficult to interpret. Either Christ is saying that He will sing the Father's praises or our praises. I choose to believe He is referring to praising the Father. If this is so, then Christ meets with us on Sunday morning and sings God's praises amid the *ekklesia (1577)*, i.e., the congregation of saints.

Song for the Day

I'll Tell the World that I'm a Christian by B.C. Fox

Thought for the Day

My two older brothers, David and Nathan Wolf, were always willing to help me when I needed help. I think Jesus is like my two older brothers in that He is always willing to help me.

Prayer for the Day

Heavenly Father, I approach Your throne today through our mediator Jesus Christ, who is my savior, sanctifier, and elder brother. Thank You for giving Your Son to suffer and die on a cruel cross to pay the price for my awful sins. Thank You, Jesus, for declaring my name in the midst of the congregation and for musicing with me to my heavenly Father. I love You, Lord, and wish to serve You throughout this life and eternal life to come. Amen.

November 10

Learning to Commit and Trust

Psalm 37:5 — "Commit thy way unto the LORD; trust also in him; and he shall bring it to pass."

This verse is telling the Christian musician to trust his or her course of life to the self-existent, eternal God who is alive, well, and able to take care of the Christian's problems. God is! He exists! He is alive! He hears our prayers! He cares! The Bible teaches very clearly that God is "touched by the feeling of our infirmities."

The Greek word *asthenia* (769) connotes feebleness, frailty and weakness. So, on the authority of God's Word, we know with certainty that the LORD is moved with compassion when He sees our weakness. God is moved, by His very nature, into action when He sees our feeble efforts to serve Him. Since we know that He cares about our "way," we need to commit our path of life unto His care.

It isn't very much fun to tell God that we are weak in some areas of our Christian walk. It is more enjoyable to ask God to send a "sin killing, world-wide revival" than to tell our heavenly Father that we have failed in some area of our life. You should not worry about being honest with our Savior, because He already knows about your infirmities. He is waiting at the right hand of the Father for you to tell Him that you are in trouble and need help knowing the way that you should walk before Him.

Remember that St. John 14:6 records that Jesus said, "I am the way..." In other words, Jesus said, "I am the road and I am the right route." So, this Scripture simply asks the Christian musician to commit his or her journey unto the LORD. I do not know what perplexes you today, but I do know that you can trust Jesus to guide you right now if you will only ask Him to help you. He will give you good directions in how to get to the Eternal City.

Prayer for the Day

I am thanking You, Lord, that You are the "way" and I am thanking You in advance for helping me to know how to walk through this sin-cursed world. Please help me to walk in Your never-failing footsteps. Lord, I know that I have many weaknesses, and some of them are so big that they could cause me to lose my way spiritually. Help me, Lord, to commit my way unto You. Please forgive me for trying to work out my problems without Your help. Help me to trust You! Help me to trust You right now to "bring it to pass." You have promised that if I will commit and trust that You will guide me every step of my life's way. These things I pray. Amen.

November 11

I Will Be With You

Isaiah 43:2 — "When thou passest through the waters, I will be with thee; and through the rivers, they shall not overflow thee: when thou walkest through the fire, thou shalt not be burned; neither shall the flame kindle upon thee."

God comforted the people of Israel because, as is stated in the first verse, "But now thus saith the LORD that created thee, O Jacob, and he that formed thee, O Israel, Fear not: for I have redeemed thee, I have called thee by thy name; thou art mine." Remember that in the thirty-second chapter of Genesis, God changed the name of Jacob (the supplanter-heel grabber) to Israel (the prince of God). Only God can change a supplanter and turn him into a prince of God.

As a Christian musician, God has changed you, and you are a child of God. Like Israel, God has redeemed you, and you are His child. It is wonderful that God claims you and says, "You are mine."

When the going gets rough, remember that God has promised, "I will be with you, and I will not let your troubles overcome you. And I will not let the fire consume you." As a matter of fact, God has promised that he will not let your fiery trials even "kindle upon you." Why? Because God has promised, "... I am the LORD thy God, the Holy One of Israel, thy Saviour... " (Isaiah 43:3). That is what our Savior does; He saves us not only from sin but also from the destruction of the fires and floods of life. These facts should help you to get a smile out of at least one side of your mouth when you are depressed. Hallelujah! Praise God! Now those of you musicians who are laboring for the Lord, out there where "the rubber meets the pavement," you must get your head up and trust God to help you have an effectual music ministry.

Thought for the Day

Christian musicians love to sing about God being the "lifter up of my head," but they do not always seem to believe what they sing.

November 12

She Shall Sing as a Door of Hope

Hosea 2:15 — "And I will give her her vineyards from thence, and the valley of Achor for a door of hope: and she shall sing there, as in the days of her youth, and as in the day when she came up out of the land of Egypt."

Bible scholars disagree as to whether this portion of the Book of Hosea is allegorical or a literal story of Hosea's unfaithful wife. Nevertheless, Hosea's name means "salvation," and this account is about salvation and restoration.

Because of forgiveness, salvation, restoration and reconciliation, Gomer was able to sing again. The word used here for sing is not the usual Hebrew word *shiyr* (7891), which simply means "to sing." The Hebrew word used here is *anah* (6030), which means not only to sing but also to respond, to pay attention, and to give an answer.

Jesus our Savior has the door of reconciliation wide open. If we have failed spiritually, He is sitting at the right hand of the Father waiting for us to repent and sing unto Him. He wants the erring musician to pay attention and to respond and give an answer with his or her whole heart. Our loving, forgiving Savior simply desires that we ask forgiveness with a repentant heart. It is a simple truth that "He's as close as the mention of His name."

Prayer for the Day

I thank You, gentle Savior, for Your loving forgiveness. Thank You that You are now sitting at the right hand of the Father praying for all musicians who have sinned and come short of the glory of God. Lord, I am asking that all those musicians that have failed spiritually will, right now, listen to the gentle voice of the Holy Spirit and will respond, repent and sing unto You. Please help them to remember that You are kind, forgiving and will not only forgive their sin, but You will also be patient with them as they seek restoration spiritually. These things I pray in Your wonderful name. Amen.

November 13

Thank God for Calvary

Luke 23:33 — "And when they were come to the place, which is called Calvary, there they crucified him, and the malefactors, one on the right hand, and the other on the left."

At Calvary
Years I spent in vanity and pride,
Caring not my Lord was crucified,
Knowing not it was for me He died
At Calvary.

By God's Word at last my sin I learned;
Then I trembled at the law I'd spurned,
Till my guilty soul imploring turned
To Calvary.

Now I've giv'n to Jesus everything,
Now I gladly own Him as my King,
Now my raptured soul can only sing
Of Calvary.

Oh, the love that drew salvation's plan!
Oh, the grace that brought it down to man!

Oh, the mighty gulf that God did span
At Calvary!

Refrain:
Mercy there was great, and grace was free;
Pardon there was multiplied to me;
There my burdened soul found liberty,
At Calvary.

—W.R. NEWELL (1895)

Thought for the Day

Have you ever thought of just where you would be today if Christ had not paid your debt of sin on Calvary?

Prayer for the Day

Thank You, Lord, that You were obedient to the will of the Father and suffered and died on Calvary's hill. I am ashamed that I didn't care enough about Your great sacrifice to love and serve You. Thank You that mercy and grace were multiplied to me. Now I tremble at the thought of Your law that I spurned. Lord, I gladly acknowledge that You are my Savior and King! Thank You for spanning the great gulf that separated me from having a personal relationship with You. Now my raptured soul sings of Calvary. Amen.

November 14

They Were Not Thankful

Romans 1:21 — "Because that, when they knew God, they glorified him not as God, neither were thankful; but became vain in their imaginations, and their foolish heart was darkened."

This is a month of harvest and thanksgiving. Today when I read this verse, it stood out to me as it never had previously.

These people were said to know God but were a people who were not thankful. It is possible that in the busyness of our musical ministry, we can get grumpy and fail to be thankful for all the many blessings that our heavenly Father has bestowed upon us.

Also, I noticed that they "became vain in their imaginations, and their foolish heart was darkened." Some Christian musicians are prone, to not only know what is wrong with everyone else, but also to constantly imagine negative things that may or may not be completely true. What came next? The Bible says that their foolish hearts were darkened. I looked up the word darkened (*skotizo* 4654) and guess what it means? It means that their hearts or imaginations became shadowed or dark. I do not want to let any negative thought to cause my thoughts to darken or obscure the spiritual light that God has given me.

Song for the Day

Come, Ye Thankful People, Come by Henry Alfred

Thought for the Day

Ephesians 4:18 — "Having the understanding darkened, being alienated from the life of God through the ignorance that is in them, because of the blindness of their heart:..." Think of it: these people were alienated from God because of blindness in their hearts.

November 15

I am Helped

Psalm 28:7 — "The LORD is my strength and my shield; my heart trusted in him, and I am helped: therefore my heart greatly rejoiceth; and with my song will I praise him."

The psalmist David expressed that his shield is the self-existent, eternal God who is alive. He also acknowledged that he received his strength from Jehovah. Sometimes church musicians only think of the struggles of public music ministry. They forget to remember and say, "I am helped." They also often forget just who it is that has helped them. When we receive help in our musicing unto God we need to practice saying out loud, "Thank You, Lord, for helping me." It will help you and Satan will not like it, because he will know that you have your head on straight.

The psalmist David acknowledged that God helped him and, since Jehovah was working in his life, he said, "My heart greatly rejoiceth." Do you rejoice when God helps you in your musicing? Do you greatly rejoice? Do you praise God, like David, with your song?

Prayer for the Day

I want to thank You, Lord, that You are my strength and shield. Thank You for helping me in my spiritual walk with You from day to day. I also want to thank You, Lord, for giving me special help with my musicing! Help me not to forget that it is You that have brought truth and joy to my life. I want to take time right now to say thank You. Now Satan knows exactly where I stand today! These things I pray in Your name. Amen.

November 16

Let's Talk about Love

1 John 4:9— "In this was manifested the love of God toward us, because that God sent his only begotten Son into the world, that we might live through him."

God knew that His Son Jesus Christ, who knew no sin, would have to die to pay the penalty for sin. That is love.

I do not understand how God could love me so much when He knew that I would reject His love time and time again.

Today is my son's (Garen Lane Wolf II) birthday. He is my son. He is my only son. He is the only son that I will ever have. I cannot explain to you how much I love him. When I think about the love that I have for him, I am reminded that I love him too much to let him die for you. So, when I think about John 3:16 — "For God so loved the world, that he gave his only begotten Son, that whosoever believeth in him should not perish, but have everlasting life" — I am mystified at how God could give Jesus up to die for sinful, rebellious men and women.

My son has made me a proud father many, many times as he grew up and became a man. He even married a lady that, in my opinion, almost walks on water. I could give you a long list of his accomplishments, but that wouldn't be very devotional or spiritual, so I will refrain from any more bragging on my only begotten son. Now you can see where I'm going with this little devotional. God spoke the world into existence. He created man and from that created being, God created woman to be a helpmate. Then God gave His Son for His creation because He loved us very much. That is so great a love that I cannot comprehend it. So, I will simply say to my Heavenly Father, "Thank You for Your great love for me!"

Scripture Thought for the Day

1 John 4:10 — "Herein is love, not that we loved God, but that he loved us, and sent his Son to be the propitiation for our sins."

November 17

Preparing to Sound

Revelation 8:6 — "And the seven angels which had the seven trumpets prepared themselves to sound."

In the Book of Revelation, at the time of the opening of the seventh seal, seven angels were given seven trumpets. The opening of the seventh seal was serious business. When the seventh seal was opened, "there was silence in heaven about the space of half an hour" (Revelation 8:1). Musicing unto our heavenly Father is serious business today. If the angels in heaven needed to prepare themselves to music in the presence of God, surely Christian musicians need to prepare themselves each time they minister in God's house.

The ministering servants in heaven were quiet before God for about a half-hour as part of their preparation for "sounding" in His presence. Likewise, we as ministering musicians must have a time of quietness in the presence of God before "sounding," i.e., musicing unto our heavenly Father. It is my opinion that public music ministering should be somewhat like an iceberg. By that I mean, there is much more hidden beneath the surface than the part the church attendee witnesses during the worship or evangelistic service.

Christian musicians spend years "tuning their harp," but many times, because they are so busy, they spend little time "tuning their heart" before ministering publically. How much time do you spend "tuning your heart" before musicing unto God? It is very important to prepare our music before we minister, but it is just as important to prepare our hearts, by practicing the presence of God, before we come before His presence with musicing.

Song for the Day

At the Name of Jesus by C.M. Noel

Thought for the Day

Before you music unto God, be sure you get quiet before the Holy Spirit so that He can talk to you about your music plans for the service.

Prayer for the Day

Lord, I want to thank You for the gift of music. Thank You that You have chosen me to be one of Your musical ministering servants. Please help me to be quiet before You so that my heart may be "tuned" to the will of the Holy Spirit for musicing unto God. These petitions I bring to You knowing that You will tune my heart if I will only turn my heart and mind toward You. Amen.

November 18

How to Conquer Your "Jericho"

Joshua 6:20 — "So the people shouted when the priests blew with the trumpets: and it came to pass, when the people heard the sound of the trumpet, and the people shouted with a great shout, that the wall fell down flat, so that the people went up into the city, every man straight before him, and they took the city."

This story of the blowing of the seven *shofarot* was given to us by the inspiration of God and therefore is profitable to us today. Just think of it — Joshua and his men of war and seven priests carrying seven trumpets (made of ram's horns) went around the city of Jericho one time a day for six days. On the seventh day (seven is the number of perfection) they went around the city six times and nothing happened. They could have stopped at this point and doubted that the extra march around the wall would make a difference. But they did as God said and went around one more time. It was on the seventh time that they went around the city that the walls fell "flat," under or even with the ground, in such a way that each soldier was able to go straight into the city.

Do you have a Jericho to conquer in your life? If so, obey God explicitly and He will give you the city. Do not only partially obey God—obey Him completely. Musicians are known to be a bit stubborn at times. You must follow God's will completely if you want Him to knock down the walls of your "Jericho."

The trumpeters blew, the soldiers shouted, and the walls "fell down flat." Whether God used the tremendous sound of the seven ram's horn trumpets or the sound of the soldiers' "great shout" to accomplish His will, or if God pushed the mighty walls of Jericho over with His little finger, is not the point of this true story. God is faithful to keep His Word if we are faithful to obey His Word and do what it says for us to do.

Thought for the Day

Sometimes we go to great lengths to try to solve our problems our way when it would be much easier to just "let go and let God have His wonderful way."

Song for the Day

Sound the Battle Cry by W.F. Sherman

Prayer for the Day

O Thou eternal, all-knowing God, help me as a Christian to hear Your voice. Help me to be faithful to Your will and Your way. Help me to believe that You will "give us the city!" for Your kingdom.

November 19

Have You Sung Unto the Lord Today?

Psalm 138:5— "Yea, they shall sing in the ways of the Lord: for great is the glory of the Lord."

Bible exegetes argue about whether this verse means "in the ways of the LORD" or "of the ways of the LORD." Although we will not settle this argument in our discussion today, I like to think it means "in." However, we do know for certain that this Scripture does command us to sing.

Have you sung unto the LORD today? The self-existent, eternal God wants you to sing unto Him. If you and I are going to make it into the Eternal City of God, we must keep our hearts singing! Even if things aren't going well, we must keep singing God's praises. I decided a long time ago to "get glad" rather than to "get mad," "get sad," "get bad," or "get even."

So, keep singing this little thought: "If you're happy and you know it, say amen." If you are going to sing in the ways of the LORD, you must sing amen— so be it. Every Christian musician goes through times of great stress and trouble. It isn't the trouble that matters; it is how you get through it that matters in the end. The LORD is very much awake, and He knows when you are in trouble. So, sing in the ways of the Lord. His way is a song of hope, triumph and victory.

Prayer for the Day

I thank You, Lord, for helping me to "sing in the ways of the Lord." Thank You for making it possible for me to get glad— even when things are not going well. I am also thanking You, Lord, for helping me to keep singing when things are far from the way that I wish them to be. Please teach me to know Your way. Teach me the right way to sing unto You when I do not feel like singing. Give me a continuous song in my heart that keeps praising You. Please help me to remember that I must sing in Your way because Your way, and glory, and power are far greater than I can comprehend. These things I pray in Your strong name. Amen.

November 20

You Must be a Partaker of the Divine Fruit

II Timothy 2:3-7— "Thou therefore endure hardness, as a good soldier of Jesus Christ. No man that warreth entangleth himself with the affairs of this life; that he may please him who hath chosen him to be a soldier. And if a man also strive for masteries, yet is he not crowned, except he strive lawfully. The husbandman that laboureth must be first partaker of the fruits. Consider what I say; and the Lord give thee understanding in all things."

Christian musician, do you regularly partake of God's divine fruit? When you are feeding others with the wonderful divine fruit produced when you music unto God, do you also partake of that fruit? If you do not, there is a distinct possibility that you may preach and feed others with your musical ministry and become weak in your own spiritual life (I Corinthians 9:27).

Here are some of the warnings and admonitions given by Timothy in this Scripture passage:

1. Endure hardness as a good soldier (vs. 3);
2. Don't entangle yourself with the affairs of this life (vs. 3);
3. Make sure you do the right thing the right way (vs. 5);
4. Be a partaker of the divine fruit (vs. 6);
5. Carefully study God's Word so that the Lord will be able to give you spiritual understanding (vs. 7).

So the heart of the matter is that you must eat if you are going to feed others. If you do not feed your own soul, you will not have an efficacious musical ministry.

Thought for the Day

Although you may not always be blessed in your soul when others are blessed by your musical ministry, you should be concerned if you are not fed, and thereby blessed, when you music unto God.

November 21

Your Spiritual Harvest

John 4:35 — "Say not ye, There are yet four months, and then cometh harvest? behold, I say unto you, Lift up your eyes, and look on the fields; for they are white already to harvest."

I grew up in Kansas, where I have observed the wonder and beauty of many wheat fields. There is nothing more beautiful than seeing a well-prepared wheat field that has just been planted. To a person that is not a farmer, it probably just looks like so much dirt. However, I know what is about to happen. In a few weeks that field will be a beautiful carpet of green. All through the cold winter that field remains a dark green. In the spring it becomes a verdant mass of green as it grows. Later in the early summer it begins to turn to a wonderful golden color as it gently waves in the Kansas, summer breezes. Then, seemingly overnight, each wheat stock bows its head with the weight of its precious content.

Now it is harvest time! I used to love to watch the golden wheat gush into the hopper of the combine as it moved slowly up and down the wheat field. When the hopper was heaped up with wheat, Dad would pull the truck up beside the combine and begin to auger the wheat into the truck as my brother and I would let the wheat pour over our bare feet.

I know that God is watching your spiritual musical harvest and, if He has feet, He is letting the results of that harvest pour over them as He looks upon the spiritual harvest, that you have been responsible for, pour into His great harvest storehouse. Zephaniah 3:17 reminds us as His servants, "The LORD thy God in the midst of thee is mighty; he will save, he will rejoice over thee with joy; he will rest in his love, he will joy over thee with singing."

Song for the Day

Now Thank We All Our God by M. Rinkart

Prayer for the Day

Dear precious Lord of the harvest, I want to thank You that You have made it possible for me to be a part of Your great spiritual harvest. Thank You that in Your great and thorough wisdom You chose to include the ministry of music in that eternal harvest. Please encourage those Christian musicians who are ministering out there where the rubber hits the pavement to complete the harvest as they remain faithful in well-doing. This I am asking You today. Amen.

November 22

Praying with Thanksgiving

Philippians 4:6— "Be careful for nothing; but in every thing by prayer and supplication with thanksgiving let your requests be made known unto God."

I must confess that I have never thought much about praying with thanksgiving until I began to study this verse in Philippians. *Eucharistia* (2169), which is translated thanksgiving in this verse, has several shades of meaning. Here is a list of meanings according to *Strong's Concordance*: gratitude; actively grateful language to God, as an act of worship, thankfulness, giving of thanksgiving. Probably most of us have come to our heavenly Father more in an attitude of complaint, fear, contrition, confession, anxiety or even sheer panic than we ever have in a spirit of thanksgiving.

The Hebrew words in the phrase "careful for nothing" *merimnao medeis* (3309 3367) connote "not even one anxiety or having no anxiety." So, we are admonished to come to our heavenly Father without any fear or anxiety. Rather, we are taught to pray with thanksgiving. This prayer attitude is in keeping with Hebrews 4:16, "Let us therefore come boldly unto the throne of grace, that we may obtain mercy, and find grace to help in time of need." Coming boldly certainly indicates trust, belief and also thankfulness. Take this day and try praying prayers of thanksgiving and gratitude to God.

Prayer for the Day

My wonderful LORD, thank You for being my Savior. You have bestowed so many wonderful blessings upon me that I am not able to even remember all of them. Thank You that I can come before You without fear or anxiety and You have promised mercy and grace in my time of need. Truly, glory and honor and blessing belong to You. Amen

Chorus for the Day

Bless His Holy Name by Andraé Crouch.

November 23

Every Day is Thanksgiving Day

I Timothy 6:6-8 — "But godliness with contentment is great gain. For we brought nothing into this world, and it is certain we can carry nothing out. And having food and raiment let us be therewith content."

Yesterday I dug potatoes from my little garden. As I got on my knees to dig them out of the ground, I soon realized that these were some of the biggest and best potatoes that I have ever raised. As I knelt there, I became very thankful to God for His material blessings. I was reminded of how wonderful God's world really is. My wife and I planted the seed potatoes in early spring in faith that they would sprout, grow and produce potatoes. I tilled the short rows of potatoes diligently, sometimes every day until the weeds were under control and the ground was prepared for the potatoes to grow properly.

As I dug the potatoes, I was reminded that God had forgiven all my sins, had planted me beside rivulets of His living water and had dug around this new Christian every day. I was reminded of just how much care my heavenly Father had taken with me so that I could be established spiritually. I am very thankful for the vegetables that God has allowed me to grow in our little garden. I am thankful for the faith of seed-time and the sight of the harvest. The tiny harvest that God has allowed me to receive from our vegetable garden has made me very thankful. It has reminded me that I should be thankful every day for all God has provided for me.

A Collect from the Book of Common Prayer

"O MOST merciful Father, who hast blessed the labours of the husbandman in the returns of the fruits of the earth. We give thee humble and hearty thanks for this thy bounty; beseeching thee to continue thy loving-kindness to us, that our land may still yield her increase, to thy glory and our comfort; through Jesus Christ our Lord. Amen."[3]

November 24

Today I am Thankful

Colossians 3:15 — "And let the peace of God rule in your hearts, to the which also ye are called in one body; and be ye thankful."

This week we celebrate Thanksgiving Day in the United

States of America. I am thankful for a day that has been set aside to thank God for His bountiful blessings that He has so freely bestowed on all of us! We all need to let God's peace permeate our hearts on this day. We are the world-wide body of Christ. To Him, we are all equal! It makes no difference how rich or poor we are or how obscure or famous we are. As Christians, we are all His children. He has forgiven us of all our sins and made us new creatures in Christ Jesus. He said in 2 Corinthians 5:17, "Therefore if any man be in Christ, he is a new creature: old things are passed away; behold, all things are become new." Praise God, I am so thankful that my old sinful life has passed away and Christ has given me a new start! I am blessed beyond measure, so I have made plans to be happy every minute of this Thanksgiving season.

Song for the Day

Come Ye Thankful People, Come by Henry Alfred

Thought for the Day

If we shared our table with someone who needs our love today, we would be a great blessing to that person. That act of unselfish love might be instrumental in leading someone else to our blessed Lord and Savior Jesus Christ.

Prayer for the Day

I am very thankful, dear Lord, that You made it possible for me to be a new creature in Christ Jesus. Lord, I do not know how to express my gratitude for the "whosoever" of the Gospel. Please accept my prayer of thanksgiving. Amen.

November 25

Musicing with Humility and Tears

Psalm 126:5 — "They that sow in tears shall reap in joy."

The Hebrew word *rinnah* (7440) is used with much latitude in the Old Testament. It often represents joy, rejoicing, shouting joyfully or singing. The Bible often speaks of the process of sowing and reaping a harvest. In this instance, one who desires to reap with the joy of singing must sow with tears.

St. Paul reminded the Ephesian elders that he had served the Lord with "humility of mind" and with many tears. Many of the problems that plague our public music ministry will never be worked out in a rehearsal or a board meeting. The Psalmist reminds us in Psalm 126 that the humility of tears will bring the desired results.

Verse 6 states, "He that goeth forth and weepeth, bearing precious seed, shall doubtless come again with rejoicing [*rinnah*, i.e., with joyful singing], bringing his sheaves with him."

The word *alummah* (485) refers to some kind of grain bound together into a bundle. In this case, it connoted the result of a spiritual harvest. If the Christian musician will have a tender "weeping" spirit, God has promised a precious harvest that will end in singing. Some things are only accomplished by prayer and humility before the Lord.

So if we, as Christian musicians, want to sing and have an efficacious music ministry, there will be a time of waiting on the Lord with humility and tears until God hears and answers our prayers. The Christian musical leader must desire the results of an efficacious musical ministry more than a music program that is flashy and showy. It takes time and continuous Spirit-led musicing before one often sees the desired results.

Thought for the Day

If you find a place of prayer, and in humility and tears cry out to God for the Holy Spirit's anointing and power, no one may ever know why your music ministry is efficacious, but you will know and God will know!

November 26

Musicians Sacrifice with the Voice of Thanksgiving

Jonah 2:9 — "But I will sacrifice unto thee with the voice of thanksgiving; I will pay that that I have vowed. Salvation is of the LORD."

Jonah sang his way out of the big fish, according to Jonah 2:8-9. He was so desperate and tired of having his own way that he began to pray and make God some promises. You would pray, too, if you found yourself in the belly of a big fish.

I heard a little chorus once at a church in Newport News, Virginia, that my wife and I attended when I was in the US Army. It went like this:

"When God tells you what to do
You'd better do it. You'd better do it.
It doesn't pay to disobey, That's all there's to it.
Like Jonah, you'll find out the hard, hard way."

If you have promised God that you will music for Him and to Him, you better pay your vow and keep ministering musically unto Him. Keep giving God your musical offering with the voice of thanksgiving. If you do not, you may find yourself in a mess spiritually.

My Bible says in Romans 11:29, "For the gifts and calling of God are without repentance." So, remember there are some things in life that you should keep doing. Why? Because God wants you to keep doing what He has told you to do. If you do not, like Jonah, you may get the opportunity to test out the acoustics inside of a big fish!

Thought for the Day

If you are gifted and called of God, the Bible says that you cannot abandon your calling and quit using your musical gifts for God.

November 27

My Soul Doth Magnify the Lord

St. Luke 1:46— "And Mary said, My soul doth magnify the Lord, and my spirit hath rejoiced in God my Saviour."

All Christian musicians should study Mary's Magnificat, or song of thanksgiving. This song is a model of Bible principles of musicing unto God. It is a good thing for Christian musicians to confess every day that "my soul doeth magnify the Lord." Christian musician, does your soul magnify the Lord at this very minute? During this busy and hectic season, is your soul rejoicing in God your Savior? How long has it been since you praised the Lord for regarding your low estate?

If anyone has anything good to say about a Christian musician, it is because the great God of heaven reached down and lifted that musician up out of a pit of noise and mire and established his or her life in Christ (Psalm 43:3).

It is the Holy Spirit who anoints our musicing in order that it may be efficacious. Mary reminds us in her song in verse fifty-four that, "He hath helped his servant Israel, in remembrance of his mercy." Praise God for this model song of thanksgiving. It would be a good idea to take time right now to thank the Lord for the musical gifts and graces that He has bestowed upon you that make it possible for you to serve Him through music.

Song for the Day

Magnificat by Keith and Kristyn Getty

November 28

The Excitement of Advent

Galatians 4:4-5 — "But when the fulness of the time was come, God sent forth his Son, made of a woman, made under the law, to redeem them that were under the law, that we might receive the adoption of sons."

The term *Advent* is derived from the Latin word *adventus* and means "the coming." Advent is observed for the four Sundays leading up to Christmas. Although some churches do not make much mention or fuss over this season, it has been observed by Christian churches since the fourth century. It is good to prepare our hearts and minds for the advent season.

Galatians 4:4-5 explains, "But when the fulness of the time was come, God sent forth his Son, made of a woman, made under the law, To redeem them that were under the law, that we might receive the adoption of sons." It is no wonder that devout Christians have counted the days of Advent with great joy for many centuries. Those who have been adopted as sons and daughters of God have a right and a responsibility to look forward to Christ's coming with exceeding great joy. So, today I start looking forward to the celebration of Christ's birthday with happiness and anticipation!

Song for the Day

Lamb of Glory by Mrs. Walter Taylor

Thought for the Day

Think about it — "When the fullness of time was come," Christ came to earth. Every Christian musician must remember that when the fullness of time has been accomplished, our loving Savior Jesus Christ will come the second time.

November 29

Christ is Really Going to Return

John 14:3 — "And if I go and prepare a place for you, I will come again, and receive you unto myself; that where I am, there ye may be also."

Jesus said that if He went away, He would come again to take us to the place that He was preparing for those who love and serve Him. It is no wonder that devout Christians get excited about the Advent season. The angels announced to the saints in the Book of Acts 1:11, "…Ye men of Galilee, why stand ye gazing up into heaven? this same Jesus, which is taken up from you into heaven, shall so come in like manner as ye have seen him go into heaven." When Jesus ascended into heaven, what was about to become a sad occasion became a blessed one because these saints were given the promise of Christ's Second Advent.

Now what are we supposed to do as we approach the Advent season? One thing is for sure, we should not waste our time writing books about the exact date that Christ will return. The nobleman of the house, just before he went away, told his servants in Luke 19:13, "And he called his ten servants, and delivered them ten pounds, and said unto them, Occupy till I come." *P r a g m a t e u o m a i* (4231), which is translated occupy here in the AV, does not mean that we should go to church and occupy a pew, but rather it means to busy oneself with the Lord's work. In the same manner, in Luke 24:46-47 Jesus said, "…Thus it is written, and thus it behooved Christ to suffer, and to rise from the dead the third day: And that repentance and remission of sins should be preached in his name among all nations, beginning at Jerusalem." So, Christian musician, you should begin in the church where you minister and in the community where you live and work. Those places are your "Jerusalem."

Song for the Day

We'll Work 'Til Jesus Comes by Elizabeth Mills

Prayer for the Day

Dear Lord, my sincere prayer is that You will make it possible for me to "occupy" until You return the second time or until You take me home to be with You in heaven. Help me to use the talents that You have given me to busy myself with the work of Your heavenly kingdom. Help me to not be weary in well-doing. This I pray in Your strong and mighty, powerful name.

November 30

Involving Children in the Advent Season

Isaiah 28:10— "For precept must be upon precept, precept upon precept; line upon line, line upon line; here a little, and there a little."

A good way to involve children in this season is to make an Advent calendar. As far as I can tell, Advent calendars can be traced back to the nineteenth century. These calendars provided a space for each day in December through Christmas Eve. Parents should make spiritual things a major part of the events which are marked in this calendar. Remember, the Bible teaches that children learn precept by precept.

The Christmas season is an excellent opportunity for children to learn about Jesus' coming and to make happy memories at the same time. Children should remember this season as a joyful time. So, make the real thing that matters during the holiday season be Christ's coming to this earth.

I remember several years ago when our family went to the Cincinnati Zoo to see the Christmas lights. It was a beautiful night, and the lights were exquisite in their brilliance, color and beauty. However, the thing I remember the most was our family riding the train and as we rounded the corner on the bridge over the pond our grandson Caiden (who was at that time just a tiny boy) burst into a portion of a song he had learned, "Here I am to worship. Here I am to bow down. Here I am to say that You're my God. You're altogether lovely, Altogether worthy, Altogether wonderful to me." Needless to say, there were tears of joy as he serenaded us that night.

Song for the Day

Children of the Heavenly Father by Caroline Sandell-Berg

Thought for the Day

In Mark 10:14, Jesus said, "...Suffer the little children to come unto me, and forbid them not: for of such is the kingdom of God." Christ was very interested in children. Take time this Advent season to include children in your pre-Christmas plans. If you do, Jesus will be pleased.

Endnotes:

1. Henry H. Halley, *Bible Handbook* (Chicago: Henry H. Halley, 1924) 551.

2. Edith Borroff, *Music in Europe and the United States*, (Englewood Cliffs, N.J.: Prentice-Hall, 1971) 4.

3. Episcopal Church. *The Book of Common Prayer and Administration of the Sacraments and Other Rites and Ceremonies of the Church, According to the Use of the Protestant Episcopal Church in the United States of America: Together with the Psalter, or Psalms of David,* (Greenwich: The Seabury Press, 1953) 265.

DECEMBER

December 1

God Was and Is in Control

St. Luke 2:1— "And it came to pass in those days, that there went out a decree from Caesar Augustus that all the world should be taxed."

Gaius Caesar Octavianus Augustus, who was the nephew of Julius Caesar, ordered a census of all the inhabitants in Judea and probably the whole land of Palestine which was under the rule of the Romans. Albert Barnes stated that "Our word tax means to levy and raise money for the use of the government. This is not the meaning of the original word here. It means rather to enroll or take a list of the citizens with their employments and the amount of their property, equivalent to what was meant by census."[1]

Therefore, Joseph was required to make the journey to Bethlehem. St. Luke 2:4 states, " And Joseph also went up from Galilee, out of the city of Nazareth, into Judaea, unto the city of David, which is called Bethlehem; (because he was of the house and lineage of David)." What seemed to be the will of man was really the fulfilling of God's will. The prophesy recorded in Micah 5:2 tells us, "But thou, Bethlehem Ephratah, though thou be little among the thousands of Judah, yet out of thee shall he come forth unto me that is to be ruler in Israel; whose goings forth have been from of old, from everlasting." The demand was official, and the human requirement was certain. However, God was working out his plan and purpose for the birth of our Lord and Savior Jesus Christ.

Song for the Day

In His Time by Diane Ball

Thought for the Day

Gaius Caesar Octavianus Augustus had a long and powerful name, but God had a greater and more powerful name.

Prayer for the Day

Lord, I want to thank You for the lesson to be learned from the census ordered by the Romans so long ago. Lord, help me somehow to see beyond the troubles of today and learn that You are still sovereign and very much in control just like You were over two thousand years ago. I want to thank You for caring as much today as You cared so many years ago when Christ was about to be born in Bethlehem. You are a wonderful God who is still ultimately in control even though the events in this world are often controlled by wicked people. Because I know that You are still the sovereign controller of the universe, I can live without fear. Thank You, Lord. Amen.

December 2

Christ has the Power to Guide Us

Isaiah 7:14 — "Therefore the Lord himself shall give you a sign; Behold, a virgin shall conceive, and bear a son, and shall call his name Immanuel."

Isaiah 9:6 promises, "For unto us a child is born, unto us a son is given: and the government shall be upon his shoulder: and his name shall be called Wonderful, Counsellor, The mighty God, The everlasting Father, The Prince of Peace." As we enter the Christmas season, we must remember that God promised that He would send Immanuel (God with us) and that He would be born of a virgin.

God also promised that "the government would be upon his shoulder." The word *shakem*, which is translated shoulder in the AV, meant that governing would be upon Christ's neck (*shakem* 7926). When we get stressed about the troubles of this world, we must remember that the government has been placed upon Jesus' neck by God the Father long before the twenty-first century. This we understand because Christ is the head of the church.

We should not forget that the Father placed upon Christ the power to be our counselor and mighty God. So Christian musicians should enter this very hectic and busy season with joy and confidence because Christ our Savior has all the power necessary to guide and direct us through the month of December.

Song for the Day

He's a Wonderful Savior to Me by Virgil P. Brock

Thought for the Day

When a Christian tries to carry a heavy load on his or her head, a tremendous amount of stress is placed on that person's neck. Most of us sooner or later cannot stand the pressure. However, we do not have to carry our burdens, because we can place all our burdens on Christ.

Prayer for the Day

Many centuries ago, You sent word that You were going to send a Savior to this sin-cursed world. Father, I want to thank You for all the many things You are to Your children. Thank You for sending the Savior of the whole world to be our Counsellor and Mighty God. Amen.

December 3

Shepherds Heard The Message First

Luke 2:8-9 — "And there were in the same country shepherds abiding in the field, keeping watch over their flock by night. And, lo, the angel of the Lord came upon them, and the glory of the Lord shone round about them: and they were sore afraid."

Can you imagine what it was like for the shepherds to be startled by an angel surrounded with the glory of the Lord shining all around the campsite? We sometimes chuckle when children and willing adults present a Christmas pageant at our local church. They all look startled when the angel, dressed in a white sheet, appears suddenly—if and when the designated deacon remembers to turn on the spotlight.

It may be a bit amusing to us, but I assure you it wasn't to those shepherds that night when they were visited by real angels. Think of it—they saw the glory of the Lord. Then the Bible account states that "…suddenly there was with the angel a multitude of the heavenly host praising God…" I believe that I would have fainted dead away at the sight of the first angel, let alone a whole bunch of them surrounded in bright shining light.

Those humble shepherds were blessed and honored by being the ones who received direct notification of Christ's birth in Bethlehem. God didn't send His angel to the "big boys" down at the synagogue, but instead He chose men that were not important to most people. If you, like me, are a nobody in this world, take time right now to praise God that He cares about the little people! Someone has said that common people must be special to God since He made so many of us.

Song for the Day

While Shepherds Watched Their Flocks by Nahum Tate

Thought for the Day

Take time today to make a list of the things that matter to you this Advent season. Ponder over the things on your list, to evaluate how many of them have lasting and eternal value.

December 4

God Sent His Angels to Mary

Luke 1:26-31— "And in the sixth month the angel Gabriel was sent from God unto a city of Galilee, named Nazareth, To a virgin espoused to a man whose name was Joseph, of the house of David; and the virgin's name was Mary. And the angel came in unto her, and said, Hail, thou that art highly favoured, the Lord is with thee: blessed art thou among women. And when she saw him, she was troubled at his saying, and cast in her mind what manner of salutation this should be. And the angel said unto her, Fear not, Mary: for thou hast found favour with God. And, behold, thou shalt conceive in thy womb, and bring forth a son, and shalt call his name JESUS."

Hebrews 1:14 explains that God's angels are ministering spirits that God sends on occasion to minister to people who are the "heirs of salvation." Certainly, Mary needed to have someone to minister to her because God's message to her was, without doubt, a shocking and seemingly impossible one. It is not surprising that the angel needed to assure her that she should not be afraid because Scripture tells us that "she was troubled" about what the angel was saying to her.

I am sure that she was shocked that the angel was saying things like, "You have found favor with God," and "You are highly favored," "The Lord is with thee: blessed art thou among women." It does not surprise me that these words were very upsetting and hard for her to understand. However, she was able to believe and submit to the will of God because God's angels are ministering spirits.

God knows just exactly what we need, and He has promised in His Word in Psalm 34:7 that "The angel of the LORD encampeth round about them that fear him, and delivereth them." God not only sends His angels to comfort and minister to very special people but also to His common musicians who love, serve and fear Him. He has promised that He will not only minister to them, but He will also deliver them from whatever troubles them. So, if you are troubled about something today, FEAR NOT, God has promised to surround you with angels that will minister, protect and deliver you! Advent should be a time of great joy—not inordinate fear.

Song for the Day

Angels from the Realms of Glory by James Montgomery

Thought for the Day

1 John 4:18— "There is no fear in love; but perfect love casteth out fear: because fear hath torment. He that feareth is not made perfect in love." God never promised that those of us who love Him would never be afraid. However, if you are a Christian musician who is often plagued with inordinate, unfounded fear, remember that God will cast out that fear, because it does not come from Him!

December 5

Astronomers on a Journey Of Faith

Matthew 2:1-2— "Now when Jesus was born in Bethlehem of Judaea in the days of Herod the king, behold, there came wise men from the east to Jerusalem, Saying, Where is he that is born King of the Jews? for we have seen his star in the east, and are come to worship him."

These wise men, who studied the stars, came from the east to worship Christ. Before Christ was born in Bethlehem, these Gentile men started their very long journey from the east. They weren't Jews, but somehow, they knew about the ancient scrolls that contained prophesies of the birth of a Jewish king. Somehow, they must have read the Isaiah scroll that stated, "Arise, shine; for thy light is come, and the glory of the LORD is risen upon thee. For, behold, the darkness shall cover the earth, and gross darkness the people: but the LORD shall arise upon thee, and his glory shall be seen upon thee. And the Gentiles shall come to thy light, and kings to the brightness of thy rising" (Isaiah 60:1-3).

These wise men understood the meaning of this passage from the Isaiah scroll with a different understanding based upon their knowledge of the study of the stars. Somehow when Christ's star appeared in the heavens at night, it sparked faith in them to seek out the Christ child and worship Him.

If God, who spoke worlds into existence, can call Gentile astronomers from the east to come to worship Christ, He can cause those in the community around your church to come to your Christmas presentation. He can make it possible for them to hear the clear message that Christ came to earth to save sinful men and women from their sins.

Chief musician, do not get discouraged. It is your job to preach Christ crucified through the musicing in your Christmas presentation, and it is the work of the Holy Spirit to convict men and women of their sin. So, go music it on the mountaintop. Tell them with your musicing that Christ was born to forgive them of their sins. You must take courage because you have a great job to do this Christmas season.

Song for the Day

Thou Didst Leave Thy Throne by Emily Elliott

Thought for the Day

Sometimes Christian musicians are afraid to try to explain the mysteries concerning the plan of salvation. Reading Scripture to those who do not understand is a powerful way to explain these mysteries. A Christian's personal testimony and effectual musicing are powerful ways to reach the lost with the gospel. The good news of the Christmas story may be the only good news that they will receive during the Christmas season.

December 6

He shall Save His People from their Sins

Matthew 1:21— "And she shall bring forth a son, and thou shalt call his name JESUS: for he shall save his people from their sins."

There are many things that Christians can and should celebrate during Advent. Among these important aspects of Christ's first and second coming, we should celebrate God's plan for everyone (John 3:16) to have forgiveness of sins. Romans 6:12-13 speaks to the issue of victory over sin— "Let not sin therefore reign in your mortal body, that ye should obey it in the lusts thereof. Neither yield ye your members as instruments of unrighteousness unto sin: but yield yourselves unto God, as those that are alive from the dead, and your members as instruments of righteousness unto God."

So many people have tried to conquer sin in their lives without God's help. All the New Years' resolutions that one can think of are no substitute for the sinner turning over his or her life to Christ. The writer of the Epistle to the Romans speaks to the issue of people "yielding" one's life to be an instrument of unrighteousness. One of the most wonderful things about celebrating Christ's coming to Earth over 2,000 years ago is his obedience to the will of the Father brought us the possibility of forgiveness of sins and peace with God. However, only those who "yield" their lives to Christ will be recipients of this peace. Try to share Christ's ability and willingness to forgive sins.

Song for the Day

Jesus Paid It All by Elvina M Hall

Thought for the Day

Acts 4:12 — "Neither is there salvation in any other: for there is none other name under heaven given among men, whereby we must be saved." Although it is popular to be pluralistic when it comes to the belief of "god," it is a fact that there is no way to be saved other than through Christ's shed blood, which is still efficacious today.

December 7

A Ruler Who Would "Feed" His People

Micah 5:2 — "But thou, Bethlehem Ephratah, though thou be little among the thousands of Judah, yet out of thee shall he come forth unto me that is to be ruler in Israel; whose goings forth have been from of old, from everlasting."

We are told that the name *Ephratah* (672) was the ancient name for Bethlehem. It means "fruitful." Bethlehem means "the house of bread." Matthew 2:6 explains, "And thou Bethlehem, in the land of Juda, art not the least among the princes of Juda: for out of thee shall come a Governor, that shall rule my people Israel." This Governor was promised to be different than the Cyrenius who was the Governor of Syria. Christ was to rule *poimaino* (4165), but this word connotes one who "feeds." So God promised that from the "fruitful house of bread," one would come one who would "feed."

Christ's first coming fulfilled the ancient promise that Christ would be a shepherd who would take care of His people. Christ's second coming will be the fulfillment that He will take care of those who love and serve him—forever.

Song for the Day

He Shall Feed His Flock from Messiah by G.F. Handel

December 8

God's Clock Keeps Perfect Time

Galatians 4:4-5 — "But when the fulness of the time was come, God sent forth his Son, made of a woman, made under the law, to redeem them that were under the law, that we might receive the adoption of sons."

For centuries the world had needed a Savior. Surely the people that were under the law were in darkness and sin. In these dark times, God the Father sent His only Son to come to earth. God knew that the wages of sin are eternal death, but God also knew that only the giving of His son Jesus could bring eternal life to this sin-cursed world. All those who loved and served YHVH during the Old Testament times looked forward to the coming of the Messiah. They must have wondered why they were left without the promised Emmanuel.

I cannot imagine what it would have been like to have been born during those dark times. The Jewish church leaders who knew the prophesies about the coming of Christ, were not looking for a Savior who would be born in obscurity, humility and poverty in a stable in the little town of Bethlehem.

But when God's clock said that it was the right time, He sent His Son to this earth to minister, suffer, die and be resurrected so that we would be able to receive remission of sins and be adopted into the family of God. Although we do not understand why the time was right for our Savior to be born, we know that he did come and that He came to save us from sin. Praise God that His clock does keep perfect time. Because it does, we are the benefactors of this great salvation.

Song for the Day

As with Gladness Men of Old by William C. Dix

Thought and Scripture for the Day

We should take advantage of this Christmas season to thank our heavenly Father for the plan of salvation. We should not forget to be thankful that, "God so loved the world, that he gave his only begotten Son, that whosoever believeth in him should not perish, but have everlasting life" (John 3:16).

December 9

God's Love for Us

1 John 4:9— "In this was manifested the love of God toward us, because that God sent his only begotten Son into the world, that we might live through him."

God sent His only begotten Son to this earth as a baby in a manger rather than as a ruler born in a palatial mansion or a conqueror who would dominate the world with great fear and power. This gift to mankind was a great demonstration of the Father's love for sinful men and women. 1 John 4:9 attests to this fact when it states, "In this was manifested the love of God toward us, because that God sent his only begotten Son into the world, that we might live through him."

As we celebrate Christ's coming to this earth, we should emphasize through our musicing and actions that Jesus suffered and died so we "might live through him." The life that our first birth affords to us is very ephemeral. Therefore we should use the short time given us for a higher purpose.

Christian musicians are well aware of St. John 3:16, but we are often not as familiar with 1 John 3:16, "Hereby perceive we the love of God, because he laid down his life for us: and we ought to lay down our lives for the brethren." As we celebrate Advent, we should remember that a Christian's life, if it is going to follow the will of Christ, is not about self but rather about others.

Song for the Advent Season

Others
> Lord, help me live from day to day
> In such a self-forgetful way
> That even when I kneel to pray
> My prayer shall be for—others.
>
> Help me in all the work I do
> To ever be sincere and true
> And know that all I'd do for You
> Must needs be done for—others.
>
> Let "Self" be crucified and slain
> And buried deep: and all in vain
> May efforts be to rise again,
> Unless to live for—others
>
> And when my work on earth is done,
> And my new work in Heav'n's begun,
> May I forget the crown I've won,
> While thinking still of—others.

Refrain
> Others, Lord, yes others, Let this my motto be,
> Help me to live for others, that I may live like Thee.
> —CHARLES D. MEIGS (1917)

December 10

They Experienced Jesus

Luke 2:20 — "And the shepherds returned, glorifying and

praising God for all the things that they had heard and seen, as it was told unto them."

I always marvel at the things that Scripture records about the shepherds. These men of faith and action went when they were told to do so, and therefore, they experienced the wonders of Christ's birth first hand. They would have missed a tremendous blessing if they had not gone to Bethlehem that night.

Because they saw Him, they came away from that humble stable "glorifying and praising God for all the things that they had heard and seen..." I am always secretly disappointed when I go to a Christmas production without spending some time around the manger. Every time I experience a manger scene, I go home rejoicing and praising God for the gift of His Son. Make sure that the audience experiences Jesus in your Christmas production this Advent season.

Song for the Day

While Shepherds Watched Their Flocks by Nahum Tate

Prayer for the Day

Dear heavenly Father, I am asking You to help me to experience the joy of Your coming during this Advent season. Help me to never lose the wonder of the miracle of the virgin birth. Help me to share my inner joy to those around me that do not know You as their personal Savior. Give me the wisdom to know how to approach others in a way that will not be offensive to them. Thank You for those who preached the message of Christ's love for me when I was just a little child. I love You, Lord, for coming to this earth to redeem me and for suffering and dying for my sin. Amen.

December 11

O Come, O Come, Emmanuel

Matthew 1:23 — "Behold, a virgin shall be with child, and shall bring forth a son, and they shall call his name Emmanuel, which being interpreted is, God with us."

During Advent, I look forward to celebrating God sending His Son to this earth. Although we do not know the exact day of Christ's birth, we can still worship Him on the 25th of December. Likewise, we have no idea when the trump shall sound in celebration and announcement of Christ's second coming, but we can still look forward with eager anticipation to the coming of Christ's kingdom when He returns for those who love and serve Him. With this in mind we can sing the Advent hymn "O Come, O Come, Emmanuel" with great joy, meaning and understanding.

The Christian knows that the thought of Christ's return to the earth is by no means "pie in the sky" but rather a "lively hope." 1 Peter 1:3 explains what Christians mean by the term "lively hope" — "Blessed be the God and Father of our Lord Jesus Christ, which according to his abundant mercy hath begotten us again unto a lively hope by the resurrection of Jesus Christ from the dead..."

Zao (2198) translated lively in the AV means living, and hence our hope is still alive and real rather than the knowledge that we believe what someone who no longer exists said when he was alive. Christianity offers this hope since we serve a God who is "I Am That I Am" (Exodus 3:14) rather than a god "who was" and now is not alive. Because Christ is alive, we have a right to worship Him with great joy and anticipation during this Advent season. I take great courage that my God, who is alive, is coming back to take me to live forever with Him.

Hymn for the Day

O Come, O Come, Emmanuel, Latin Hymn

Thought for the Day

Revelation 22:20— "He which testifieth these things saith, Surely I come quickly. Amen. Even so, come, Lord Jesus." Spend some time today thinking about the fact that Christ said, "Surely I come quickly."

December 12

The Long Journey to Bethlehem

Luke 2:4-5— "And Joseph also went up from Galilee, out of the city of Nazareth, into Judaea, unto the city of David, which is called Bethlehem; (because he was of the house and lineage of David:) To be taxed with Mary his espoused wife, being great with child."

Mary and Joseph's long trek from Nazareth to Bethlehem was a journey of faith. Caesar Augustus had decreed that all the people should be registered, or "taxed." Joseph's journey with Mary was not merely an act of obedience to Caesar Augustus but also to God. The angel had assured Joseph that he should not be afraid to accept Mary as his espoused wife.

Mary and Joseph completed their journey to Bethlehem the evening before the birth of our Savior Jesus Christ. Because he trusted God, Joseph was not ashamed of Mary. Joseph was willing to sign the tax register and publicly accept Mary as his espoused wife—going on record for all eternity that he trusted and believed God. It took great faith and trust in Mary and in God for Joseph to believe what the angel had revealed to him about Christ's birth.

Are you among the Christian musicians that trust God? Are you willing to trust God with your life, your career, your future and your music ministry? Trust comes with implicit faith in God that He will guide you and protect you for the rest of your life. Joseph's implicit faith that the angel of God had told him the truth enabled him to take the long journey to Bethlehem. It will be by faith alone that you will enter the New Year knowing in your heart that God is saying to you, "Be not afraid."

Song for the Day

O Little Town of Bethlehem by Phillips Brooks

Thought for the Day

It is one thing to say that we trust God with the "journey," but it is another thing to start walking!

Prayer for the Day

Lord, I know that You will never fail me or lead me astray. Give me the courage and strength to keep on my journey of musicing for You and to You. I believe that You have placed me exactly where I am "for such a time as this." Please guide my musical ministry and help me to reach out to Your strong arms for protection. Lord, like Joseph I am willing to trust Your will and Your path for me for the rest of my life. I love You Lord. Please help me to keep ministering musically for Your glory. Amen.

December 13

No Room for Jesus

St. Luke 2:7 — "And she brought forth her firstborn son, and wrapped him in swaddling clothes, and laid him in a manger; because there was no room for them in the inn."

Can you imagine that there was actually no room for the Son of God at the inn in Bethlehem? Many times we as musicians have a hard time understanding why bad things happen to good people. Mary, Joseph and the baby Jesus were undoubtedly good people. Why did God the Father let Jesus, His only begotten Son, be born in a cattle shelter which was perhaps a cave? From our very finite understanding, it would seem that there could have been at least a tiny room that no one was using. However, God the Father let His only Son be born in obscurity and humility. As we approach this blessed day of days, we should remember that, regardless of our circumstances, most of us were not born in a place of humility like Jesus.

Jesus didn't let his surroundings and his humble birth ever affect His ministry. Likewise, His earthly parents did not let the humility of the circumstances of Christ's birth affect their vision of who Jesus was and their role in the accomplishment of the will of God. Thank God for Mary and Joseph, who did not let their situation deter them from obeying God that wonderful night long ago in Bethlehem.

Song for the Day

Away in a Manger, anonymous

December 14

Now We Know "The Rest of the Story"

St. Luke 2:17-18— "And they [the shepherds] came with haste, and found Mary, and Joseph, and the babe lying in a manger. And when they had seen it, they made known abroad the saying which was told them concerning this child."

God trusted the message of the coming of the Savior with the shepherds first. When I read this passage of Scripture, I am reminded of why God trusted them with the good news that Christ had been born in Bethlehem that night.

First of all, the Scripture tells us that they did not mess around about seeking out the Christ child, but rather they "came in haste" to find Him. They did not doubt the word of the angel that He had been born in a manger. They were simple people with a simple faith that made them God's choice to hear and see first.

Second, after they had seen and heard, they went back to the mountains and "…made known abroad the saying which was told them…" God knew that they would go and tell it on the mountain that Jesus Christ was born to save sinners. Their reaction was to "go and tell," which was much different than Herod's "go and kill."

Third, St. Luke 2:20 tells us that, "And the shepherds returned, glorifying and praising God for all the things that they had heard and seen, as it was told unto them." God chose the shepherds because He knew that they would not only worship Christ at the manger but that they would go home and give Christ true worship by telling everybody they met that the Messiah was indeed born to save sinners.

So, we should learn from this three-part lesson that we, like the shepherds, should "taste and see" that Christ is good. We should go home and tell everyone unashamedly that Christ was born to save lost men and women. Finally, our musicing should give glory to God as we tell the good news of Christ's birth.

Song for the Day

Joyful, Joyful, We Adore Thee by Henry van Dyke

Thought for the Day

Have you ever wondered why people who have been recently saved usually are the ones who light a fire under a sleepy church?

December 15

"In Dulci Jubilo"

John 3:16 — "For God so loved the world, that he gave his only begotten Son, that whosoever believeth in him should not perish, but have everlasting life."

The Latin hymn "*In dulci jubilo,*" i.e., "Good Christian Men
Rejoice," was written in the fourteenth century. It was translated into English by John Mason Neale in 1818. The words
that touch my heart in this Christmas hymn are, "Now ye
need not fear the grave." Why do we not need to be afraid?
Because "Jesus Christ was born to save!" Who will He save?
This wonderful hymn declares that He "Calls you one and
calls you all to gain his everlasting hall." Thank God, because of the 'whosoever' of the Gospel, none of us have to
miss the joys of heaven! If you cannot rejoice when you read
this text—you can if you will only give your life to Him.
Below are the words of this wonderful old Latin hymn.

> Good Christian men, rejoice - with heart and soul
>   and voice;
> Give ye heed to what we say: Jesus Christ was born
>   today.
> Ox and ass before him bow, and he is in the man-
>   ger now.
> Christ is born today! Christ is born today!

> Good Christian men, rejoice—with heart and soul
>   and voice;
> Now ye hear of endless bliss: Jesus Christ was born
>   for this!
> He has opened heaven's door, and we are blest
>   forevermore.
> Christ was born for this! Christ was born for this!

> Good Christian men, rejoice—with heart and soul
>   and voice;
> Now ye need not fear the grave: Jesus Christ was
>   born to save!
> Calls you one and calls you all, to gain His everlast-
>   ing hall.
> Christ was born to save! Christ was born to save!

Thought for the Day

Real joy does not come to the musician who knows the particulars of Christ's birth, but rather to the musician who knows Christ in a particularly personal way.

December 16

The Unwanted Gift

Proverbs 17:17 — "A friend loveth at all times, and a brother is born for adversity."

Romans 1:11 — "For I long to see you, that I may impart unto you some spiritual gift, to the end ye may be established."

Today is my oldest brother Dr. David Wolf's birthday. Thinking about his birthday has caused me to remember a gift that he gave me many years ago. We all like to receive gifts, but this gift was different. It was a beautiful and expensive gift, but that did not matter to me because I did not want to receive it. It is what I call the unwanted gift. I cannot remember when he gave it to me, but I will never forget that he brought it with him when he came home from the US Navy. The unwanted gift was a Bible.

The reason that I did not want it was because I was not a Christian at that time and had no intention of reading it. David has given me many fine gifts over the years, but this was the greatest gift that he has ever given to me. That is saying a lot because he once gave me a car! The Bible was a great gift because it brought me face to face with my lost condition. It made me think about the fact that I was very sinful and needed to confess my sins and give my heart to God.

There was an even greater gift that was given to sinful men and women—that gift was God's giving of His only Son Jesus Christ to come to this sinful world to live, suffer and give His life on a cruel cross at Calvary. Many sinful men and women have not yet received that wonderful gift, but thanks be to God, He gave His only begotten Son to die for them. My brother gave a gift to me because he loved me. God gave His only Son for sinful men and women because He loved us all with a wonderful, unfathomable love. Make sure that you tell someone about this amazing gift during this Advent season.

Song for the Day

Oh Come All Ye Faithful, Eighteenth Century Hymn

Thought for the Day

As the Christmas season is now here and you will be giving gifts to others, try to give gifts to your unsaved friends and family members that will cause them to think about their lost spiritual condition.

Prayer for the Day

Dear Lord, I want to thank You for giving me an older brother that loved me enough to give me, what was at that time, an unwanted gift. I want to also thank You for giving Your son to pay the awful penalty for my sins. I also want to thank You for sending the Holy Spirit to convict me of the awfulness of my sinful life. Because of two unwanted gifts, I am Your adopted son today. Thank You for caring for my soul. Amen.

December 17

In the Will of God at Christmas

Jeremiah 1:5— "Before I formed thee in the belly I knew thee; and before thou camest forth out of the womb I sanctified thee, and I ordained thee a prophet unto the nations."

Today is my firstborn daughter Deanna's birthday. At the time I am writing this devotional, she is thousands of miles away from us. She is a navy chaplain's wife in the British Royal Navy. Before she was born, God knew who she was and what He wanted her to be doing right now. He sanctified or "set her apart" and ordained her to be a minister's wife who would go to the nations.

You may have loved ones who are ministering far, far from home today. You and I need to constantly be reminded that God is awake. Nothing slips up on Him. There is no luck or happenstance, and nothing startles God because, in His awesome wisdom, He always knows what is best.

I would rather have my children thousands of miles away from me, serving God, than to have them all around my table but out of the will of God for their lives. With that in mind, we will celebrate the birth of God's Son Jesus Christ with joy and full confidence that He is working out His purpose in our lives. My heavenly Father sent His only Son to die. I only sent my daughter to serve Jesus Christ.

Song for the Day

Hark the Herald Angels Sing by Charles Wesley

Thought for the Day

It is one thing for parents to bring a baby to an altar in a church and dedicate that infant to the Lord, but it is another thing to still be willing for the Lord to have His way in that person's life when he or she is getting on an airplane to fly thousands of miles away to serve the Lord.

December 18

God Really is with Us

Isaiah 7:14 — "Therefore the Lord himself shall give you

a sign; Behold, a virgin shall conceive, and bear a son, and shall call his name Immanuel."

St. Matthew 1:23 quotes Isaiah's prophesy and further explains that Emmanuel means "God with us." To a people long ago who were in great darkness, God promised to send His Son to be with us! It was a long time after Isaiah's prophesy before Christ was born of a virgin in Bethlehem, but God always keeps His promises.

Christian musician, be sure to remind everyone who takes part in your Christmas musical ministry that Christ's coming to earth, in space and time, was a fulfillment of God's promise to mankind that God really would come to earth to dwell with us. Although you, as a music minister, may believe that all those who minister musically with you know all about the story of Christ's coming to earth—tell them again!

I get blessed just thinking about the fact that God was and is with us. We are not alone on this earth. We may not be able to see Him, but we can experience His presence very, very near us at this time of Christmas. Christ came to abide with us—not just visit us. He came to tabernacle with his children. Be sure to invite all who minister with you to experience Christ in a special way as they music unto Him. Experiencing His presence will make their musicing real and very special this Christmas season.

Song for the Day

It came upon the Midnight Clear by Edmund H. Sears

December 19

It Wasn't Just Any Baby

Luke 2:12— "And this shall be a sign unto you; Ye shall find the babe wrapped in swaddling clothes, lying in a manger."

I was looking at the second chapter of Luke's gospel, and this verse stood out to me. I wonder what went through these shepherd's minds when the angel proclaimed, "You shall find *the* baby." The angel wasn't talking about just any baby. This baby was the Son of God. These men were keeping the night watch over their sheep so that wild animals would not kill them. I have often wondered why God sent one of His angels to these humble, hard-working men.

Although I have no evidence to prove my theory, these men must have been knowledgeable of the prophecies concerning Christ's birth. Luke 2:11 tells us that the angel announced to these men, "For unto you is born this day in the city of David a Saviour, which is Christ the Lord." They had no doubt been looking for the Messiah to come, but it is somewhat unlikely that they thought that He would be born at that time. During this Advent season Christian musicians believe that Jesus will return someday, but many busy musicians are not looking for Him to come today or tomorrow.

Song for the Day

Come, Thou Long-expected Jesus by Charles Wesley

December 20

Wise Men Came to Worship Christ

Matthew 2:1-2 — "Now when Jesus was born in Bethlehem of Judaea in the days of Herod the king, behold, there came wise men from the east to Jerusalem, Saying, Where is he that is born King of the Jews? for we have seen his star in the east, and are come to worship him."

We do not know when the kings came to Jerusalem, or when they appeared at Joseph and Mary's home. It is generally believed that it was about a year after Christ's birth. There is much conjecture about just who these Eastern Magi were. Many believe that they were philosophers. There is some possibility that they were Jews of mixed descent who lived in distant lands and were knowledgeable of the Messianic prophesies in the Jewish Scrolls. If so, then they could possibly have believed that the time of Christ's coming was at hand.

Since they followed Christ's star, it is possible there were astronomers among them –and thus the statement, "We have followed his star." However, the thing that mattered was that they traveled all those miles to worship Christ. They believed that He was the "king," so they diligently sought after Him. They believed that they would indeed find the Christ child. Even more importantly, it is apparent that they believed that He was the Messiah and that He was worthy of their worship.

Hebrews 11:6 states, "But without faith it is impossible to please him: for he that cometh to God must believe that he is, and that he is a rewarder of them that diligently seek him." Wise men and women still seek Him. In their seeking, it is still necessary for them to believe, like the wise men who sought after Christ; and they must believe, not only that he is, but that he will reward those who seek him with salvation.

Song for the Day

The First Noel, Traditional English Carol

Thought for the Day

If a musician wishes for his or her musicing during the Christmas season to be efficacious, he or she should spend more time with Him. Those who know God are able to music much more effectively for Him than those who merely know a lot about God.

December 21

I Have Access to God's Grace

Matthew 1:21— "And she shall bring forth a son, and thou shalt call his name J ESUS: for he shall save his people from their sins."

Think of what Joseph thought when he realized that "she was found with child of the Holy Ghost" (Matthew 1:18) and that… "He shall save his people from their sins" (vs.21). I am sure that Joseph's mind was in a whirl as he contemplated Christ's birth. I am glad that both Mary and Joseph were willing to obey God.

Because of their obedience, they were able to be used in the Father's great plan of salvation. I am so thankful for a perfect covenant that made it possible for my sins to be forgiven. Why wouldn't I be happy during this Christmas season? "Therefore being justified by faith, we have peace with God through our Lord Jesus Christ: By whom also we have access by faith into this grace wherein we stand, and rejoice in hope of the glory of God" (Romans 5:1-2). So, I will be rejoicing in the "the glory of God" because by faith, I have been given access to God's saving grace.

Song for the Day

There's a Song in the Air by Josiah G. Holland

Thought for the Day

Because the Christian musician is justified by faith in Jesus Christ, he or she has peace and daily access to God's grace. There are many means of grace available to the believer. Do take advantage of them during this Advent season.

December 22

Being Ready at Christmas

I Corinthians 15:52 — "In a moment, in the twinkling of an eye, at the last trump: for the trumpet shall sound, and the dead shall be raised incorruptible, and we shall be changed."

A Christmas Nightmare
'Twas a night in December when Christ returned to this earth.
And although 'twas near Christmas we weren't thinking of His birth.
We were all worn out 'cause things had been popping.
Our family was all preoccupied with Christmas shopping.
The children were all in bed that night.
My wife and I had just had a big fight.
When all of a sudden I heard Christ's trumpet sound,
I ran to the front door with a big bound.
Although I had fully planned at the trumpeter to yell,
When I was surrounded with light to my knees I fell.

Christ took the book from the angel that night,
As He searched for my name there I gasped in fright.
I knew He'd not find it on those pages that night,
For in my heart there were things I had not made right.
I fell on my knees that fateful night,
It caused me to make sure that my heart is right.

Although you now know that this whole poem is
   fake,
I hope it will cause you right choices to make.
                              —GLW

December 23

Only Two More Days

Mark 8:38— "Whosoever therefore shall be ashamed of me and of my words in this adulterous and sinful generation; of him also shall the Son of man be ashamed, when he cometh in the glory of his Father with the holy angels."

Today is the 23rd of December. Everyone is advertising that there are only two more shopping days until Christmas! What would happen if we as Christian musicians were that open and showed the same kind of urgency about people knowing our Lord Jesus Christ? What impact would it have on those around us if we were to tell them that there are only two more days to find our precious Lord as Savior if they are going to have a personal relationship with Him this Christmas? It is time for Christians to take Christ with us to the public arena.

During the Christmas season, Christian musicians have a wonderful opportunity to take the good news of the gospel to those who are unchurched. Everyone is out shopping, and they are not surprised or offended when they hear singing in public places. Matthew, Mark, and Luke all instruct Christians to "go ye." St. Matthew states explicitly, "Go ye therefore, and teach all nations." Every time I go into a shopping mall during the Christmas season, I am impressed at the diversity of cultures and nationalities that are represented. Christian musician, you should find some public venue where you can sing and play about the goold news of Christ's comings to "all nations."

Song for the Day

I Heard the Bells on Christmas Day by Henry W. Longfellow

Thought for the Day

With only two more days until we celebrate Christ's birth, if you haven't already, it is time to start planning ways to make the 25th of December a blessed day. Think of ways to honor and bless Jesus Christ this Christmas.

December 24

Making Preparations

Mark 8:36— For what shall it profit a man, if he shall gain the whole world, and lose his own soul?

The Night Before
'Twas the night before Jesus returned to this earth,
And people were stirring all over this earth.
Christmas parties and programs took everyone's
   time,
But all this commotion brought none peace of
   mind.
Many church pews were empty for few could find,
A moment for worship or His honor at this time.
We wanted to change things, for we all well knew,
That if we did what was needed, there was much
   repenting to do.
We had good intentions and made plans anew,
To make good on resolutions and follow them
   through.
If we could reverse time as we look back,
We would do more than say we were on the wrong
   track.

We would change our thinking and our actions
    fast,
And make preparations for the life that will last.
    —GLW

Song for the Day

Silent Night by Joseph Mohr

December 25

What Christmas Day Means to Me

Isaiah 9:6 — "For unto us a child is born, unto us a son is given: and the government shall be upon his shoulder: and his name shall be called Wonderful, Counsellor, The mighty God, The everlasting Father, The Prince of Peace."

Today is December 25th, and it is the very exciting day that many have been looking forward to celebrating. Today is the day that we celebrate the first coming of our Savior who is: Wonderful, Counsellor, Mighty God, Everlasting Father and the Prince of Peace. I have been contemplating just what all these names of God mean and also what the coming of our Savior on this Christmas Day means to me. Certainly it reminds me of the old, old story of Christ's birth in Bethlehem over 2,000 years ago, where He left the portals of heaven to come to this sin-cursed world. Christmas means that Jesus Christ was obedient to the will of His Father by coming to earth. Christmas also means that provision was made for this Kansas farmer to have his sins forgiven and spiritual life in Christ. I not only have spiritual life, but this life in Christ can be and is an abundant life!

Song for the Day

Joy to the World by Isaac Watts

Thought for the Day

It is not too late to include Christ in Christmas, even if He has been pushed to the side by legitimate things. Today is His birthday so you can celebrate His coming. Start by reading the Christmas story to your family before you open gifts.

December 26

Christ's Coming Brought Us Everlasting Life

John 11:26 — "And whosoever liveth and believeth in me shall never die. Believest thou this?"

God the Father sent His Son, to not only suffer and die for all of us, but also that we may have everlasting life because, as John 3:16 explains, "For God so loved the world, that he gave his only begotten Son, that whosoever believeth in him should not perish, but have everlasting life." Wow! That is a happy thought to begin this day after Christmas. I want to stress that in Christ Jesus we all can have everlasting life. Now that does not mean that we will not die someday, but it does mean that if we are born-again, we have God's promise of everlasting life.

So, we should begin this day after Christmas with the joyful thought that when we are in Christ, we have everlasting life. God the Father gave us the most wonderful gift that has ever been given to mankind. He gave His only begotten Son! 1 John 4:9 reminds us all that, "In this was manifested the love of God toward us, because that God sent his only begotten Son into the world, that we might live through him." That is surely a very happy thought. We who are in Christ Jesus actually have life through Him!

Chorus for the Day

Emmanuel by Bob McGee

Thought for the Day

Today is the day after all the hustle and bustle of Christmas. Contemplate the fact that He will be with you today and every day of this year.

December 27

The Wise Men Saw Jesus

St. Matthew 2:11 — "And when they were come into the house, they saw the young child with Mary his mother, and fell down, and worshipped him: and when they had opened their treasures, they presented unto him gifts; gold, and frankincense and myrrh."

The wise men did not stop until they had come all the way to the house where Jesus was. They didn't come part of the way, but rather they came all the way to find Jesus. When they were in the presence of Jesus, they were able to worship Him.

If we are going to truly worship Jesus, we must get past the earthly palace of Herod, past the dusty road of problems that we encounter on our journey to worship, and past all the distractions that would keep us from coming into His presence. We must take the journey from the natural to the supernatural if we intend to come into his presence. We can only truly worship Christ when we are in His presence.

The magi believed in the authenticity of the Christ so much that they "fell down" before Him. Notice that it was after they fell down before Him (they prostrated themselves before Christ) that they presented gifts to Him. This signifies that we must give Christ our hearts and worship before we are able to give gifts to Him. The grateful magi gave Him the emblematic gifts of gold, frankincense and myrrh. Adam Clarke stated that they "offered Him the things which were in most esteem among themselves…"[2]

If we are going to truly worship Christ, we should

present to Him the things we esteem the most. We value our time, our money and our lives. It is easy to offer prayers and say and sing words of honor, but it is a different thing to dedicate our time, money, ambitions and talents to Him! The greatest gifts that we can give to Christ are a willing heart and our time. If we are going to bring these gifts to Him, we must let Him remove all sin and submit our heart to Him so that He can purify us through and through. We must also give Him our bodies as living servants.

Song for the Day

All the Way by Rodney Griffin

Thought for the Day

Jesus came all the way to earth for us. How far are we willing to go for Him? He gave His life for us. How much of our lives are we willing to give for Him?

December 28

Forgiving Others

St. John 1:14 — "And the Word was made flesh, and dwelt among us, (and we beheld his glory, the glory as of the only begotten of the Father,) full of grace and truth."

Surely Jesus was full of grace and truth because, if we had received what we deserved, it would have never been forgiveness. Isaiah 40:2 states, "Speak ye comfortably to Jerusalem, and cry unto her, that her warfare is accomplished, that her iniquity is pardoned: for she hath received of the LORD's hand double for all her sins." I am sure that I deserved to receive double punishment for my sins. I do not like to talk about my former sinful acts. They were many and most grievous.

We are reminded in Ephesians 4:32, "And be ye kind one to another, tenderhearted, forgiving one another, even as God for Christ's sake hath forgiven you." I want to be sure to be kind to someone that may not merit my kindness. I remember that Romans 6:23 declares emphatically, "... the wages of sin is death; but the gift of God is eternal life through Jesus Christ our Lord." Maybe I should start by being sure that I have forgiven one of my former renters who left owing me several month's rent.

Scriptural Thought for the Day

Ephesians 4:32— "And be ye kind one to another, tenderhearted, forgiving one another, even as God for Christ's sake hath forgiven you."

Colossians 3:13— "Forbearing one another, and forgiving one another, if any man have a quarrel against any: even as Christ forgave you, so also do ye."

December 29

The Whole Year Through

Romans 5:8— "But God commendeth his love toward us, in that, while we were yet sinners, Christ died for us."

The Whole Year Through
So remember while December
Brings the only Christmas Day
In this year let there be Christmas
In the things you do and say;
Wouldn't life be worth the living?
Wouldn't dreams be coming true?
If we kept the Christmas spirit
All this whole year through?
—ANONYMOUS

This little anonymous poem is a good motto as we see the end of December and head into the New Year. The spirit of Christmas is encapsulated in the golden text of the Bible, John 3:16— "For God so loved the world, that he gave his only begotten Son, that whosoever believeth in him should not perish, but have everlasting life." There are two words in this text that are worth our consideration as we enter this New Year.

First, there is the word loved (*agapao* 25), which means charity or unselfish love in action. Certainly, God's sending of His only begotten Son to save sinful men and women who did not love God was an unselfish action and the greatest action of love.

Second, there is the word gave (*didomi* 1325) which is used in the NT in a number of applications. It means literally to give, but it also means to commit, to yield, to bestow and to give for suffering. All of these meanings represent what God did for us when He gave us His only Son.

So, this little poem should help to guide our actions as we love and give to others during this New Year. This humanistic culture purports that we should all exert our will on others. It teaches that we should get all that we can get and "can" all we get during this year. The example of the spirit of Christmas is to give the very best that we have to this sin-cursed world. I do not know what you have to give to others, but whatever you have should be shared with those who need it most. St. Matthew 10:42 recorded the words of Jesus—"And whosoever shall give to drink unto one of these little ones a cup of cold water only in the name of a disciple, verily I say unto you, he shall in no wise lose his reward."

Song for the Day

Because I Have Been Given Much by Kittie Suffield

Prayer for the Day

I want to thank You, my heavenly Father, for loving and giving unselfishly. Thank You for giving us Your only Son. Thank You for making provision for my salvation and the salvation of the whole world. Thank You for not being willing for any of us to perish, but rather willing that we should all repent of our sins and accept Your love for us. I am asking You, Lord, to help me to keep the spirit of Christmas throughout this New Year. This I pray in Your loving name. Amen.

December 30

The Holy Spirit Was Upon Simeon

St. Luke 2:25 — "And, behold, there was a man in Jerusalem, whose name was Simeon; and the same man was just and devout, waiting for the consolation of Israel: and the Holy Ghost was upon him."

It is a great testimony left behind by Simeon, attested to by St. Luke, who wrote under the inspiration of God, that Simeon was a just (*dikaios* 1342) and devout (*eulabes* 2126) man. Simeon was just in that he was innocent before God and therefore a holy man. He was also called a devout man because he walked circumspectly before God and therefore was a religiously pious man.

Simeon was a person whom God trusted so much that He promised Simeon that he would see the Christ before he died. We have further evidence that Simeon was a holy man in that the Scripture states very clearly that "the Holy Ghost was upon him." Even before the dispensation of the Holy Spirit was ushered in at the Day of Pentecost, Simeon was said to be holy because the Holy Ghost was upon him.

This man who lived a holy life was able to not only see the Christ child but also able to take Him up in his arms and proclaim with great faith in chapter two verse 30, "For mine eyes have seen Thy salvation." Praise God, as Simeon proclaimed in verse 32 that Christ was "A light to lighten the Gentiles, and the glory of thy people Israel." Praise God that this verse takes me in because I am a Gentile. Christ not only came for His own, but also for all the rest of us who required, in our lost and alienated condition, to be adopted as sons and daughters of God.

Song for the Day

And Can it Be by Charles Wesley

Thought for the Day

God is still seeking holy men and women to go and tell His message of Christ's salvation.

December 31

Get Thee Up Into the High Mountain

Isaiah 40:9— "O thou that tellest good tidings to Zion, get thee up into the high mountain; O thou that tellest good tidings to Jerusalem, lift up thy voice with strength; lift it up, be not afraid; say unto the cities of Judah, Behold your God!" (KJV Cambridge Ed. margin)

The responsibility of Zion was to not only "go tell it on the mountain" but to tell it with all their might. We know this because this verse states, "lift up thy voice with strength." We as Christian musicians are responsible, to not only music the message of Christ's coming to this earth, but to also at times to do it at a double *forte*. Furthermore, we are responsible not to be negative about the good news. People are lost and in need of Jesus Christ our savior. They are hungry to have peace in their hearts, and some of them will respond to the gospel message.

Finally, we are admonished to say unto the people to whom we minister, "Behold your God." Although they may know that they are lost, they need us to go to the high mountain and shout the message that Christ has come to save them from their sins. All Christian musicians who have the privilege of musicing the gospel during this Christmas season, and in the new year that starts tomorrow, must remember that they are telling good tidings of great joy to all those who hear the message of Christ's coming to earth to save sinful men and women.

Song for the Day

Tell Me the Story of Jesus by William H. Parker

Thought for the Day

God is telling all those who know Him to tell others the glad tidings of the import of Christ's birth.

Prayer for the Day

I want to thank You, Lord, for giving me the privilege of hearing the good tidings of the significance of Christ's birth. Thank You for giving Your Son because You loved me when I was far from You. Please help me to music Your message as long as You give me breath. These things I am praying in Your wonderful and faithful name. Amen.

Endnotes:

1. Albert Barnes, 16.
2. Adam Clarke, 46.

BIBLIOGRAPHY

Vol. 1: January-June and Vol 2: July-December

Allen, Clifton J. *The Broadman Bible Commentary.* Nashville, Tennessee: Broadman Press, 1973.

Barnes, Albert. *Barnes' Notes on the New Testament.* Grand Rapids: Baker Books, reprinted 1998.

Barnes, Albert. *Barnes' Notes on the Old Testament.* Grand Rapids: Baker Books, reprinted 1998.

Borroff, Edith. *Music in Europe and the United States.* Englewood Cliffs, N.J.: Prentice-Hall, 1971.

Carter, Charles W., Ralph Earle, and W. Ralph Thompson. *The Wesleyan Bible Commentary.* Grand Rapids, Michigan: William B. Eerdmans Pub. Co., 1986.

Clark, Adam. *Clarke's Commentary.* 6 Vol. Nashville: Abingdon Press, n.d. (Now published by Schmul Publishing Co.)

Davidson, Benjamin. *Analytical Hebrew and Chaldee Lexicon of the Old Testament.* MacDill AFB, Florida: MacDonald Publishing Company, n.d.

Delamont, Vic. *The Ministry of Music in the Church.* Chicago: Moody Press, 1980.

Episcopal Church. *The Book of Common Prayer and Administration of the Sacraments and Other Rites and Ceremonies of the Church, According to the Use of the Protestant Episcopal Church in the United States of America: Together with the Psalter, or Psalms of David.* Greenwich: The Seabury Press, 1953.

Godbey, W. B. *Godbey's Commentary.* Cincinnati, Ohio: Revivalist Press, 1898.

Grimm, Wilke S. Translated, revised and enlarged by Thayer, Joseph H. (*Clavis Novi Testamenti) The New Thayer's Greek-English Lexicon of the New Testament.* Peabody Mass., Hendrickson Publishing, 1981.

Halley, Henry H. *Bible Handbook.* Chicago: Henry H. Halley, 1924.

Harper, A.F., ed. *Beacon Bible Commentary.* 10 Vol. Kansas City, MO: Beacon Hill Press, 1969.

Harris, R. Laird, ed. *Theological Workbook of the Old Testament.* Chicago: Moody Press, 1980.

Henry, Matthew. *Matthew Henry's Commentary.* Mclean, VA: MacDonald Publishing Company, n.d.

Idelsohn, A. Z. *Jewish Music: In Its Historical Development.* New York: Tudor, 1948.

Jamieson, Robert, A.R. Fausset, and David Brown. *Commentary: Critical and Explanatory on the Whole Bible.* Grand Rapids, Michigan: Zondervan Publishing House, 1950.

Johansson, Calvin M. *Strengthening Church Music in the Evangelical Church.* Bloomington, Indiana: West Bow Press, 2019.

Kittel, Gerhard, ed. *Theological Dictionary of the New Testament.* 10 Vol. Grand Rapids: Wm. B. Eerdmans Publishing Company, 1976.

Leadership Ministries Worldwide. *The Outline Bible Five Translation: Practical Word Studies in the New Testament.* Chattanooga, TN: Leadership Ministries Worldwide, 1998.

Lenski, R.C.H. *Interpretation of St. Matthew's Gospel.* Peabody, Mass: Hendrickson, 1998.

Poole, Matthew. *Matthew Poole's Commentary on the Holy Bible.* Mclean, Virginia: Macdonald Publishing Co., n.d.

Pritchard, Ray. *Names of the Holy Spirit.* Chicago: Moody Publishers, 1995.

Sachs, Curt. *The Rise of Music in the Ancient World, East and West.* New York: Norton, 1978.

Spence-Jones, H.D.M., Joseph S. Exell, and Edward Mark Deems. *The Pulpit Commentary.* Mclean, Va.: MacDonald Publishing Co., 1980.

Strong, James. *The New Strong's Exhaustive Concordance of the Bible.* Nashville, TN: Thomas Nelson, 2010.

Tregelles, Samuel, trans. *Gesenius' Hebrew and Chaldee Lexicon of the Old Testament.* Grand Rapids: Wm. B. Eerdmans Publishing Company, 1949.

Haik-Vantoura, Suzanne; Translated by Dennis Webber, edited by John Wheeler. *The Music of the Bible Revealed.* Berkeley: Bibal Press, 1991.

Vincent, Marvin R. *Vincent's Word Studies in the New Testament.* 4 Vol. Peabody, MA: Hendrickson Publishers, n.d.

Vine, W.E., Merrill F. Unger, and William White. *Vine's Expository Dictionary of Biblical Words.* Nashville: Nelson, 1985.

Wesley, John. *Explanatory Notes Upon the Old Testament.* Grand Rapids, Michigan: Baker Book House, 1986.

Wigram, George. *Analytical Greek Lexicon of the New Testament.* Wilmington, DE: Associated Publishers and Authors, Inc., n.d.

Wigram, George. *The New Englishman's Greek-English Concordance of the New Testament.* Wilmington, DE: Associated Publishers and Authors, 1976.

Wigram, George. *The New Englishman's Hebrew and Chaldee Concordance.* Wilmington, DE: Associated Publishers and Authors, 1975.

Wolf, Garen. *Music of the Bible in Christian Perspective.* Salem, OH: Schmul Publishing Company, 1996.

Wolf, Garen. *Church Music Matters.* Salem, OH: Schmul Publishing Company, 2004.

Wolf, Garen. *Music Philosophy in Christian Perspective,* Nicholasville Kentucky: Schmul Publishing Company, 2018.

Made in the USA
Monee, IL
31 May 2021